DECORATING WITH FABRIC

DECORATING WITH FABRIC

*More than 40 beautiful projects
for your home*

for Melissa and Billy

• DIANA CIVIL •

a Salamander book

**Published by Salamander Books Limited
LONDON**

A SALAMANDER BOOK

Published by
Salamander Books Ltd
129-137 York Way
London N7 9LG
United Kingdom

© 1996 Salamander
Books Ltd

Distributed by
Random House Value
Publishing, Inc.
40 Engelhard Avenue,
Avenel, New Jersey 07001

A CIP catalog record for
this book is available from
the Library of Congress.

ISBN 0 517 15948 1

1 3 5 7 9 8 6 4 2

◆

EDITOR
Helen Stone

COPY EDITOR
Marion Elliot

PHOTOGRAPHER
Russell Sadur

STYLIST
Diana Civil

ILLUSTRATOR
Nicola Gregory

DESIGNER
Graham Mitchener

COLOR SEPARATION
*P&W Graphics Pte Ltd,
Singapore*

FILMSET
*Creative Text Ltd,
London*

Printed in China

CONTENTS

INTRODUCTION

Fabric is a versatile medium. It has the capacity to completely transform the look of a room by evoking mood and bringing colour and comfort. By making your own furnishings, you can bring a style to your home which is completely your own.

The thought of making home furnishings may be a daunting one but, in practice, you will find that all manner of projects can be made using just basic skills, yet achieving successful and professional results.

Each of the projects in this book is designed to be made using just a few simple sewing stitches and some even employ quick and easy methods such as using glue or a staple gun. These projects are perfect for those on a limited budget or with limited time, as they are quick and simple to make but look good, allowing you to obtain wonderful results with the minimum of effort and outlay.

Even with the more elaborate furnishings, you will find that construction is a simple and straightforward process of stitching seams in a logical sequence, so don't be deterred from making something that looks ornate. If you take the time to measure and cut out fabric accurately, all kinds of projects can be undertaken, from small finishing touches and simple chair throws to more ambitious items like curtains, fitted chair covers and a patchwork quilt.

▼ *Fabric can be used to create an individual look in every room. The colours and styles of the fabric that you choose will affect the feel of the room and you can use this to best advantage creating warm, inviting living rooms and light, clean bathrooms.*

Whatever you decide to make, it is satisfying to feel that you are adding a personal and creative touch to a room.

An important part of ensuring successful results is good forward planning. Some projects are suitable for working on over a period of time but with others, such as a pair of lined curtains, it is better to set aside an afternoon to enable you to cut out all the fabric pieces in one go. You will also need to clear adequate space when making projects which require large amounts of fabric and gather together all the materials you need to complete the job.

You may like to make several co-ordinating items such as matching curtains and cushions or a tablecloth and napkin set. These extra finishing touches will make your home special and will give you a real sense of achievement. With just a little imagination, you can adapt the projects in this book to suit many styles of decor, using fabrics which reflect your personal taste. There is a wide range of beautiful furnishing fabric available in a variety of colours, patterns and weights. Look for interesting and unusual fabrics to create an individual look.

Soft furnishings can be made plain or can be decorated with piping, braiding, embroidery or fringing, but you will find that the same basic method of construction applies whatever your chosen finish.

Above all, this book is designed to encourage the novice and the more experienced alike to have the confidence and creativity to carry out a whole range of projects and to search out fabrics which inspire. It shows ingenious ways of creating soft furnishings which can be adapted to fit in with your own home; after all, the home is a reflection of the owner's personality.

▽ *In addition to the more general home furnishings such as curtains and cushions, there are innovative ideas which enable you to transform a plain room. Bedrooms for both adults and children can be given a dramatic focus by framing a plain bed with a canopy.*

1

BASIC TECHNIQUES

The key to creating professional-looking home furnishings is to use a suitable fabric and a tried and tested technique. Before tackling any of the projects in this book, it is a good idea to familiarize yourself with the basic techniques that you will need to use.

The following pages include useful information about suitable fabrics, the correct way to measure up for curtains and blinds, the appropriate stitches to use and the different accessories available. Using the techniques described will ensure that making each project is a straightforward process and, once mastered, will enable you to achieve successful results time after time.

1·1 KNOWING FABRICS

Selecting an appropriate fabric is probably the most important part of any home furnishing project. As well as different weights, fibres and textures, there are hundreds of patterns and colours to choose from.

When choosing a fabric, your main concern should be that your choice is suitable for the item you are making. Chair covers, cushions and sofa throws all require hard-wearing fabrics, whereas table linen needs to withstand regular washing. Read the labels on fabric samples to check the composition, instructions for care and to look for any special properties such as a stain-resistant or fade-resistant finish.

Cost may also affect your choice, particularly if a project requires a lot of fabric. Attempting to create a sumptuous effect with a meagre amount of material is a false economy and a more professional finish can be gained using a more generous amount of a cheaper fabric.

Colour and pattern
The fabric needs to suit not only the item being made, but also the shape and size of the room and its contents. The function of a room and the way you occupy the space are of prime importance as colour and pattern can have a transforming effect.

Strong or dark colours and patterns may look bold and dramatic on the roll but, in practise, they will instantly make a room feel smaller and more enclosed. Pale colours and soft shades emphasize light and will open out the proportions of a room.

The use of pattern can also transform a room and so care must be taken to chose patterned fabric in proportion to the object being made. Subtle patterns may appear prominent close up but then can disappear from sight at a distance, whereas bold florals can be overpowering, making a room look smaller and cluttered.

Creating a co-ordinated look
When mixing patterns you should aim to link key elements such as shape, colour or scale. Contrast patterns and plains will sit well together if they are complimentary shades or colours.

Basic equipment
For most home furnishing projects, a basic sewing kit should provide all the necessary equipment. Check that you have everything you need before beginning each project.

Here are the most useful items:
Good scissors
A large pair of dressmaking scissors as opposed to household scissors are necessary for cutting fabric. You should also have a small pair of scissors for snipping threads and for delicate work. If you intend to work a lot with fabric, it is worth investing in a good pair of pinking shears.
Non-stretch fabric tape measure and retractable steel tape
These are vital, as accurate measuring is of the utmost importance.
Dressmaking pins
It is worth investing in steel pins as they do not mark the fabric or leave holes.
Needles
A wide variety of needles are necessary for use with different threads and materials.
Tailor's chalk
This is useful for marking out fabric, especially when making piping strips.
Thread
Always match both the colour and weight of thread to the fabric you are working with. Leftover lengths of thread at the end of a reel can be used for tacking.
A sewing machine
A sewing machine is not vital for soft furnishings, but it certainly makes the job easier and quicker. A standard sewing machine should have all the stitches you need to complete most projects.

POINTS TO CONSIDER WHEN BUYING FABRIC

■ Look at the fabric in daylight as well as artificial light to check that it is the exact colour you require. You may find that the colour changes dramatically in artificial conditions.

■ Gather up a length of fabric from the roll to assess how it drapes or creases and whether it is suitable for its intended use. For upholstery projects, the fabric must be robust, for curtains it must have good drape and, for cushions, be firm but comfortable.

■ If in any doubt as to whether the fabric is the correct weight or weave, check with the shop or manufacturer.

■ Examine the fabric to check for flaws. A supplier should give you additional fabric to compensate for any flawed pieces.

■ Always buy enough fabric to complete your furnishing project as finding the same material can not only prove difficult, but colour can vary dramatically between batches.

■ However attractive, do not be tempted to use dress fabrics for any furnishing purposes other than as trimmings, as these do not stand up to prolonged use.

◀ *Pattern and colour can be used to visually alter the proportions of a room. Stripes generally make a room appear taller (top left), whereas dark colours and boldly patterned furnishings can make a room appear smaller and more enclosed (top right). Pale colours can be used to emphasize light and space (left).*

1·2 MEASURING UP

Accurate measuring is a vital step in achieving a neat and professional finish for any home furnishing project. It is important to double check the sizing before buying and cutting fabric to avoid expensive and time-consuming mistakes.

For the most common items such as curtains, blinds, cushions, covers and tablecloths, there are standard procedures for measuring which remain relevant no matter which style you choose.

When measuring, use a non-stretch tape with metal ends or, for large areas, use a retractable metal tape measure. Take your time and write down each measurement as you go. If you are in any doubt, check and check again.

Calculating curtain width

The width of fabric for curtains and blinds is generally based on the length of the curtain track or pole rather than the window frame itself. It is also affected by the type of heading tape used, as different tapes require different fullnesses of fabric.

To allow maximum light into the room, it is a good idea to extend the track or pole beyond the window frame as this allows the curtains to be drawn right back so they are clear of the glass.

To determine the width of the curtains, measure the track or pole once it has been fitted in position. This is the basis of your calculation so remember to allow a little extra if the curtains are to overlap in the centre. Multiply this measurement $1\frac{1}{2}$, 2 or $2\frac{1}{2}$ times depending on the heading tape chosen (see page 19). You may need to join widths of fabric to achieve this measurement and these should be joined along the selvedges, using a small seam allowance.

Calculating the desired length

To determine the length, you must first decide whether the curtains are to be sill-length, floor-length or to create a generously draped effect on the floor. You also need to allow for the heading tape to cover or stand slightly above the curtain track. If you are

hanging the curtains from a decorative pole, they should hang just clear of the pole, leaving it visible. Measure the depth from the point where you estimate the top of the curtain will be to the point representing the finished length. Add allowances for the top turning and lower hem. The top turning allowance is generally 4cm ($1\frac{3}{4}$in) when a

POINTS TO CONSIDER

■ Fabric with a strong repeating pattern must be cut and joined very carefully. Centralize the pattern on each curtain.

■ If you can't avoid cutting through a horizontal motif, place the partial repeat at the bottom of a floor length curtain where it will not be noticed.

■ Save offcuts from pattern matching to make tiebacks, a valance or cushions.

◀ *Make a window seem taller by hanging the track significantly higher than the frame (top left). To add width, extend the track either side of the frame (left). Add both height and width to make the window seem larger overall.*

▼ *Fabrics with strong horizontal patterns should be cut to give a complete motif at the top and bottom of the curtain (below).*

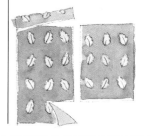

heading tape or facing is used, but allow more if you are making a gathered heading with a frill standing above the tape. The bottom hem is generally 15cm (6in) for unlined curtains and 10-15cm (4-6in) for lined curtains.

To work out the total fabric allowance, divide the total width of both curtains by the width of your chosen fabric. Round up this amount to the next whole number, creating an allowance for seams and side hems. Divide the figure in two to find out the number of full-width fabric pieces in each curtain. This will also tell you whether a half-width is needed on either side. The number of drops multiplied by the cut length is the total amount of fabric you need to buy. Add extra for pattern matching if necessary.

Measuring up for lining fabric

Although lining fabric is generally plain so no pattern matching is necessary, you should allow the same amount of lining as for the main curtain fabric.

Café curtains

Measure the area of window to be covered and add 4cm (1³/4in) to the width for side hems. Add 12cm (4³/4in) to the length to allow for a hem at the bottom and a casing at the top which will thread onto the curtain wire or rod (this measurement should be adjusted to accommodate your particular style of curtain rod).

For a frilled café curtain, multiply the width measurement 1¹/2-2 times to create the fullness in the curtain.

Measuring up for blinds

A blind can be positioned inside or outside the window recess but, if the blind is to be teamed with curtains, it should hang inside. Fitting a blind outside the recess can compensate for a window that is not quite square at the corners or, alternatively, can be used to make a small window look larger. Blinds that are fitted inside the window provide a neat, streamlined look but, before making up your blind, check that it is feasible to mount the brackets,

track or batten onto your window frame and that any window catches or locks will not obstruct the movement of the blind.

Roman blind

Measure the required width and add 4cm (1³/4in) for side seams. Add 11cm (4¹/2in) to the drop for top and bottom turnings.

Roller blind

Add 2cm (³/4in) to the measured width for side hems and 20-25cm (8-10in) to the drop for a lath channel at the bottom and attachment to the roller at the top.

Festoon blind

Measure the width of the track and multiply by 1¹/2-2¹/2 depending on the type of heading tape used (see page 19). Add a small allowance for side seams and any fabric width joins. For a lightly-ruched blind, allow twice the measured length of the recess from track to sill and, for a fuller effect, allow three times the length; the allowance for top turnings and hem are included in this measurement.

Austrian blind

The width should be calculated in the same way as a festoon blind. For the length, add 6cm (2¹/2in) to the required drop for hems and top turnings.

A gathered café curtain adds a soft touch to a window and provides privacy whilst letting in some light. The curtain should measure 1¹/2-2 times the width of the window to allow for sufficient gathering.

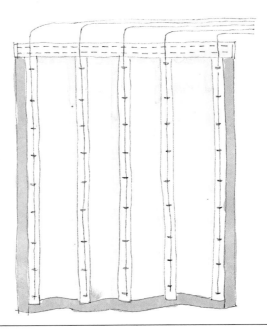

Roman, festoon and Austrian blinds are made by more or less the same method, using differing amounts of fabric. A Roman blind is generally measured to fit the width of the window, whereas an Austrian or festoon blind will require 1¹/2-2¹/2 times the width of the window in fabric to create soft or full gathers. The differing effects are created by the use of corded tapes sewn in parallel lines down the length of the blind (left).

Measuring up for tablecloths

Whatever the shape of your table, you will find that you can measure for a tablecloth in much the same way; the measurements you need to take are the dimensions of the tabletop and the drop of the tablecloth.

The ideal drop of a tablecloth is one which is comfortable when you are sitting at the table. If it is too short, the cloth will have a skimped appearance; too long and the cloth will be draping in your lap as you dine. Generally, a drop of around 25-30cm (10-12in) is about right. When measuring, remember to take into account the depth of any borders, frilling or fringing you plan to add to the finished cloth.

Unless designed to have a contrasting border or trimming, tablecloths should ideally be made from a single piece of fabric. If your table is large, you may need to seam widths of fabric together. To achieve the best results, make a central panel with equal side panels, seaming along the selvedges of the fabric. This applies to both rectangular and round cloths.

Circular tablecloth

Measure the diameter of the tabletop and add twice the depth of the drop plus 3cm (1¹/4in) for hem allowances to this measurement. You will need to begin with a square of fabric which you can then fold into quarters before cutting the cloth to a circular shape.

Rectangular or square tablecloth

Measure the length and width of the tabletop. To each measurement, add twice the drop from the edge of the table, adding 6cm (2¹/2in) for hem allowances.

Measuring up for cushions

When measuring up cushion covers, you can use the cushion pad as a template. Measure the width and height of the cushion pad then simply add the required allowances for seams and fastenings.

Square cushion

To calculate the amount of fabric necessary for a square cushion cover, measure the

length and width of the cushion pad and add 1.5cm (³/4in) allowances to each seam.

Circular box cushion

Measure the diameter of the cushion pad and add a 3cm (1¹/4in) seam allowance to this measurement. For the gusset, measure the depth of the pad and its circumference, adding 3cm (1¹/4in) to both measurements.

Bolster cover

The simplest bolster cushion cover is constructed from one piece of fabric, gathered over the circular ends. To calculate the depth of the fabric required, measure the length of the cushion pad plus the diameter of the circular end. For the width, measure around the circumference of the cushion pad, then add 3cm (1¹/4in) to each measurement for seam allowances.

◀ *For a round table, measure the diameter of the tabletop, then add twice the overhang to this measurement (left). For a rectangular cloth, measure the width and length of the tabletop and add twice the overhang (bottom, left).*

▼ *Measure across the width and depth of a square cushion, adding seam allowances (below).*

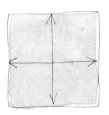

▼ *For the gusset on a round cushion, measure the circumference of the pad and the required depth (below).*

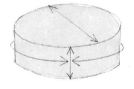

▼ *Measure the length and diameter of a bolster to calculate the length. The width is equal to the circumference (below).*

▶ *You will need to make a paper pattern for any type of fitted seat cushion (right).*

A fitted bolster cover, in which the shape is more defined, is made from three separate pieces of fabric. It has a rectangular section for the main body and two circular pieces which fit the ends. For the main piece, measure the length of the bolster and its circumference, adding seam allowances. For the ends, cut two circles each with the same diameter as the bolster pad with added seam allowances.

Fitted seat cushions

To measure for a fitted seat cushion, you will first need to make a template of the chair seat; this is easy to do using a sheet of tracing paper or brown paper.

Lay the paper on the seat and, holding it in place with one hand, draw around the seat edge using a pencil. Add 1.5cm (³/4in) seam allowances on all sides and mark in the position of any uprights.

A basic cushion can be made by cutting two pieces of fabric to the shape of the template, sewing them together and filling this with wadding; this will give a relatively flat pad. For a thicker pad, use thicker wadding or a foam pad and insert a gusset into the cushion fabric. The depth of the gusset should be gauged from the thickness of the foam pad, adding a seam allowance.

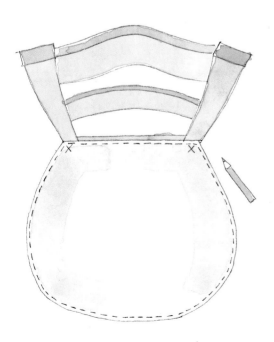

For the width, measure the circumference of the cushion template and add a 3cm (1¹/4in) seam allowance.

Tie-on frilled chair cushion

Make a paper pattern of the seat in the same way as for a fitted seat cushion, marking the position of the uprights.

To calculate the amount of fabric required for the frill, measure around the front of the chair from one back strut to the other and multiply this measurement 1¹/2 times. For the back frill, measure between the two back struts, again multiplying this measurement by 1¹/2. The depth of the frill is a matter of taste but, as a standard measure, 13cm (5in) provides a generous looking frill without being impractical.

For the ties you will need two strips of fabric measuring 1m x 13cm (40in x 5in).

Fitted chair cover

A cover which encases the entire chair can be made from two pieces of fabric; the main piece covering the seat pad and the backrest from the front of the seat to the floor at the back of the chair, and the second piece forming a skirt which fits around the perimeter of the chair. If your fabric is patterned, the main section should be made from two pieces of fabric which are seamed at the top of the backrest. This allows the pattern to run the correct way up on either side of the backrest.

For the length of the main piece, measure from the front edge of the seat pad and across the seat. Continue this measurement up the front of the backrest and down the other side to the floor. Add 3cm (1¹/4in) for seam allowances. For the width, measure the width of the chair at its widest point and add 3cm (1¹/4in) seam allowance.

For the length of the frill, measure around the seat of the chair from back leg to back leg and add a 3cm (1¹/4in) narrow seam allowance. Multiply this measurement 1¹/2 times for gathering. For the depth, measure from the edge of the seat to the floor and add a 1.5cm (¹/2in) seam allowance for a bottom hem and 2cm (³/4in) for gathering at the top.

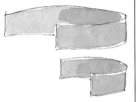

▲ The frill for a seat cushion should be made in two sections. Measure between the two back legs of the seat for the shorter piece and around the front of the seat for the longer. Both these measurements should be multiplied 1¹/2 times (above).

▲ For the main section of a fitted chair cover, measure from the front of the seat to the floor at the back of the chair (above).

1·3 STITCHES AND SEAMS

A variety of stitches are used when making home furnishings and these can be created by hand or machine. Each stitch has its own particular uses and it is worth familiarizing your self with the most common.

Machine stitches

Although most home furnishing projects can be made by hand, using a sewing machine will certainly make the job quicker and easier. The most basic sewing machine will be capable of all the stitches necessary to make the projects in this book.

Straight stitch *fig 1*

This is the most widely used stitch for joining two pieces of fabric. It is suitable for all materials except stretch fabrics.

Top stitch *fig 2*

Top stitch is a form of decorative stitching which is machined on the right side of the fabric, often with two spools of thread. It can comprise of straight, zigzag or embroidery stitches.

Zigzag stitch *fig 3*

This is most commonly used to finish raw edges or for decoration. When using for finishing, the length and width of the zigzag must be set carefully to ensure that the stitching prevents fraying; the stitches should be as small and narrow as possible.

If used for decoration, zigzags can range from narrow to widely spaced.

Hand stitches

Even if you use a sewing machine, there are still many techniques which require hand stitching using a needle and cotton.

Gathering/Running stitch *fig 4*

This hand-worked stitch is ideal for gathering frills. Work a row of small, neat, evenly-spaced stitches near the edge of the fabric, leaving the threads dangling at one end. Sew a second row of stitches 6mm (¹/4in) below the first in the same way. Pull up the loose threads to gather the fabric.

Basting or tacking stitches

These stitches are made in a similar way to running stitch but they should be longer and looser. A useful stitch called 'even basting' is used to hold two or more layers of fabric together or to mark single layers. Knot the end of the thread to start and work along the fabric with long, even stitches. Use slightly shorter stitches around the curves and finish with one backstitch. Remove the basting by gently pulling the starting knot.

Oversewing *fig 5*

This stitch is mainly used for neatening raw edges by hand and consists of a line of stitches looped over the edge of the fabric.

Backstitch *fig 6*

Backstitch creates an imitation machine stitch by hand. After each forward stitch, the following stitch is sewn back to meet it. This creates a line of continuous stitches.

Hemming stitch *fig 7*

This stitch is used for hand sewing a hem in place. Fasten the working thread inside the hem and make small slanting stitches through the fabric and the hem in one movement. Pick up one or two fabric threads with the needle at each stitch and space the stitches evenly across the hem.

Whip-stitch *fig 8*

This is a tiny hand stitch used to join two edges or to attach a trimming to a fabric edge. With right sides facing and raw edges even, secure the working thread on the edge nearest to you. Take the needle diagonally over both edges and bring it through to the front very close to the top, picking up a few fabric threads. The stitches should be small and very close together.

fig 1 Straight stitch

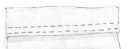

fig 2 Top stitch

fig 3 Zigzag stitch

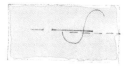

fig 4 Running stitch

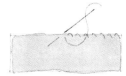

fig 5 Oversewing

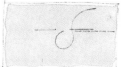

fig 6 Backstitch

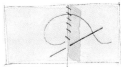

fig 7 Hemming stitch

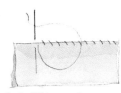

fig 8 Whip-stitch

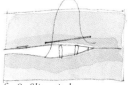

fig 9 Slip-stitch

Slip-stitch *fig 9*

This stitch is used to join two folded edges together with an invisible stitch. Fasten the thread inside one folded edge then cross over the opening to the opposite fold. Make a stitch about 6mm (^{1}/4in) long and pull the needle through into the other fold again. Continue working backward and forward across the gap.

Lock stitch *fig 10*

This stitch is used to hold lining material in place on the reverse of curtains and is sewn in vertical columns at regular intervals along the curtain width. With the lining pinned in position on the fabric, fold the lining back and make small stitches along the fold, picking up just one or two threads of the fabric. Before the needle is pulled through the fabric, the thread should be brought round under the front of the needle to create a loop.

Seams

There are two basic types of seam: the functional seam which holds two pieces of fabric together and the decorative seam.

Straight seam/Open seam *fig 11*

This flat, neat seam can be used in most instances with the exception of fine materials which fray easily or gathered fabrics. The two pieces of fabric are stitched together with right sides facing and raw edges matching. The seam allowance is then opened out and pressed flat.

French Seam *fig 12*

This seam is suitable for sheer fabrics or those which fray easily. The raw edges are enclosed within the seam, making it unsuitable for thick fabrics. The fabric is placed wrong sides facing and seamed. The seam allowance is then trimmed and the fabric is flipped over to bring the right sides together. A second seam is sewn, encasing the first.

Flat fell seam *fig 13*

This durable seam is used on home furnishings which are laundered regularly.

Place the fabric pieces with right sides facing and pin and stitch a straight seam. Press the seam allowance to one side. Trim the underneath allowance to 6mm (^{1}/4in). Fold the top allowance over, enclosing the trimmed edge. Press the fold flat and pin and stitch it to the fabric close to the edge.

Piped Seam *fig 14*

A piped seam has matching or contrasting covered piping cord inserted between the two main pieces of fabric to provide a focal point and a neat, tailored finish. It is not suitable for use with soft, draped fabrics, but a softer effect can be achieved by inserting fabric piping strips without the piping cord. The piping is sandwiched between two layers of right-facing fabric, with the raw edges of fabric even. All the layers of fabric are then seamed at once, using the straight seam method.

Bound seams *fig 15*

Bias binding or strips of bias cut fabric can be sewn into the seam in the same way as piping to create a neat, tailored finish.

Top stitched seam *fig 16*

Any seam can be decorated with top stitch, worked in matching or co-ordinating thread. This additional stitching will strengthen the seam as well as giving a decorative finish.

Neatening raw edges

The raw edges of a hem should be neatened to prevent the fabric from fraying. This can be done in several ways:

Zigzag *fig 17*

Using zigzag stitch, work over the raw edges of the seam allowance.

Oversewing *fig 18*

The edges of the seam allowance can be oversewn by hand with small, neat stitches.

Binding

Raw edges can also be bound with shop-bought binding. The binding is folded over the raw edge and stitched in place.

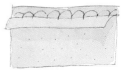

fig 10 Lock stitch

fig 11 Open seam

fig 12 French seam

fig 13 Flat fell seam

fig 14 Piped seam

fig 15 Bound seam

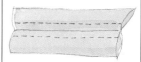

fig 16 Top stitched seam

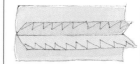

fig 17 Zigzag

fig 18 Oversew

1·4 HEMS AND HEADINGS

Hems and headings are important elements in most furnishing projects. They are not only used to neaten edges and give a professional finish, but can also affect the way in which a fabric falls and prolong the life of your furnishings.

Almost all soft furnishing projects will need raw edges hemming at some stage and you should aim to choose the most suitable hem for the fabric and type of project. The depth of the hem can vary but it should always be kept in proportion to the scale of the item.

Hems can be stitched either by hand or machine but the main aim is to enclose and neaten the raw edge and provide a neat, tailored look to the item. Mitring is a neat way to finish deep hems at corners and this solves the problem of thick folds of fabric in each corner which may make the fabric hang badly.

Simple hemming stitches
Straight stitch *fig 19*
This is a simple way to hem using a straight machine stitch. Fold and press the hem, then position the machine foot on the fold so that the needle enters the double thickness of fabric 5mm (^{1}/4in) away from the folded edge. Stitch across the width of the hem. Reverse stitch on your sewing machine to finish off.

Zigzag stitch *fig 20*
This is an overcasting machine stitch which can be varied on the machine to suit the type of fabric used. Stitches can range from short and narrow to long and wide. When hemming, the bulk of the zigzag should be on the folded fabric.

Blind hem stitch *fig 21*
This can be worked on a sewing machine or by hand and provides a combination of straight stitch and zigzag stitch. If sewing by hand, fold back the hem edge and fasten the thread inside it. Sew a small stitch in the fabric about 5mm (^{1}/4in) along, then sew a small stitch in the hem 5mm (^{1}/4in) to the left. Continue sewing in this way,

alternating between fabric and hem all the way along.

Herring-bone stitch *fig 22*
Working from left to right (if right-handed), secure the thread in the folded fabric. Pick up a couple of threads from the flat fabric with the needle pointing from right to left. Pull the thread through. Position the needle further to the right still pointing it to the left and take a horizontal stitch through the folded fabric.

Slip hemming *fig 23*
Working from right to left (if right-handed), secure the thread in the folded fabric. Catch the flat fabric and insert the needle inside the folded edge. Slide the needle along for approximately 5mm (^{1}/4in). Bring the needle out of the fold and catch a couple of threads from the flat fabric at the point where the needle emerged.

Mitring *fig 24*
Mitring the corner where two hems meet reduces the bulk of the fabric and creates a neat finish to projects such as curtains, tablecloths and napkins.

To mitre a corner, make a single hem fold along one edge then turn under a single hem along the adjacent edge. Press both hems in place. Unfold the fabric and turn the corner over so that the diagonal fold passes exactly through the corners of the hemline creases. Trim off the excess fabric at the corner leaving a 5mm (^{1}/4in) seam allowance turned over.

Turn in the hems along the hemline creases, making sure that the corners are folded accurately. Press and pin these in place before stitching along all the hems and slip-stitching the diagonal seam where the two hems meet.

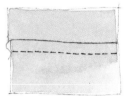

fig 19 Straight stitch

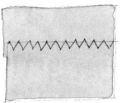

fig 20 Zigzag stitch

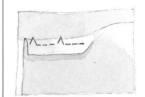

fig 21 Blind hem stitch

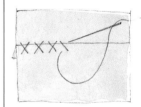

fig 22 Herring-bone stitch

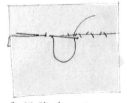

fig 23 Slip hemming

fig 24 Mitring

Headings

There is a wide range of heading tapes available in different materials and styles to suit all kinds of curtains and blinds. Your choice of tape can make the world of difference between a plain or a stylishly opulent window treatment.

A heading tape has cords threaded through it which are used to gather up the curtain fabric and it is the differing arrangement of the cords which is responsible for the finished effect.

The design of the tape is also the key to how much fabric you will require to make up your curtains and this can vary quite dramatically. Choose your heading tape carefully to ensure that you have the most suitable type for your project.

Standard heading *fig 25*

This narrow tape is used mainly on small, lightweight curtains and creates a simple, gathered heading. It requires $1^1/2$-2 times fabric fullness.

Pencil pleat heading *fig 26*

This tape requires $2^1/4$-$2^1/2$ times fabric fullness and creates neat, regular pencil-effect pleats at the top of the curtain.

Pinch pleat heading *fig 27*

Stylish and elegant, pinch pleat tape creates a fanned effect at the top of the curtain and requires 2 times fabric fullness.

Box pleat heading *fig 28*

This decorative heading tape is ideal for curtains and valances which remain in a fixed position. Box pleat tape requires 3 times fabric fullness for elegant draping.

Smocked pleat heading *fig 29*

Suitable for valances or fixed curtains, this tape creates a traditional 'smocked' effect at the top of the curtain. It requires $2^1/2$ times fabric fullness.

Alternative ideas

The use of heading tape gives a traditional look to the headings of curtains and blinds. However, alternative headings can be used ranging from tied and tab heads, to clips and draped fabric effects. Tied and tab headings may be knotted, looped or attached to rings which are threaded onto the curtain pole. Although simple and effective, these type of headings do not slide smoothly and are more effective as a decorative finish rather than a practical one.

As a modern alternative in a contemporary setting, experiment with clothes pegs or curtain clips to peg a length of fabric to a tension wire fitted in the window recess.

Pelmets

Pelmets give a neat, professional finish to the tops of curtains and blinds and are simple to make and economical with fabric.

When making a pelmet, it is important to consider its size in proportion to the room and whether it balances with the style and length of the curtains.

A fabric pelmet generally consists of three layers: a top fabric, a lining material and a stiffener. The layers are bonded or sewn together, then fixed above the window on a pelmet board or shelf. Buckram is a suitable stiffener for most projects or, for speed and ease, a self-adhesive pelmet stiffener is a good alternative.

For large, shaped pelmets, plywood or MDF (medium density fibreboard) is a more suitable choice. This can be cut to shape using a jigsaw and then nailed onto a sturdy pelmet board above the window.

Valances

A valance is a miniature curtain which hangs over the top of the window to provide a frame to the curtains. It can be soft and draped, gathered, shaped or stiffened but, whatever the style, it should always be in proportion to the curtains, window and the scale of the room. As a general guide, a valance should be at least $1/6$th of the drop of the curtains.

A valance should be hung from a special valance track which can be added to a standard curtain track or you can buy a dual purpose track which hangs both curtains and valance simultaneously.

fig 25 Standard

fig 26 Pencil pleat

fig 27 Pinch pleat

fig 28 Box pleat

fig 29 Smocked pleat

▲ *A valance provides a neat finish to the top of a curtain. For a balanced effect, its size should always be kept in proportion to the curtain, the window and the room (above).*

1·5 FINISHING TOUCHES

The addition of carefully-chosen trimmings and other accessories to plain furnishings can transform the functional into the decorative, evoking a mood of glamour, grandeur or simple chic.

Finishing touches can make your home furnishings really special. Piping the seams of a plain cushion can add glamour, a fringed edge will give a pelmet grandeur, and even a plain hem on a tablecloth or napkin can be shaped using pinking shears to give it instant 'designer style'.

The most common trimmings include piping, binding, braids and ribbons, and there are also other useful finishing touches to consider such as buttons, beads, bows and tassels which can be used to co-ordinate a number of furnishings in a room.

When buying trimmings, check that they are pre-shrunk and colourfast and buy sufficient to allow for working around corners and neatening ends.

Pinking

This is one of the simplest ways of adding a decorative edging and is ideal for smaller items such as cushions and tablecloths. Pinking shears have serrated blades which cut a zigzag effect into the edge of the fabric. However, they are not suitable for use on fabrics which fray.

Piping

Piping is a strip of bias cut fabric which is inserted into a seam giving a neat, defined finish. It can be either flat or corded with the bias cut strips of fabric wrapped around a length of piping cord. Corded piping is available in various thicknesses.

Covered piping *fig 30*

It is easy to make your own covered piping. To cut the bias strips, fold a piece of fabric so that the selvedge lies parallel with the straight grain of the fabric and cut off the triangle of excess fabric. To calculate the required width of the strips, measure the circumference of the piping cord and add a double seam allowance. Mark the width of the strips on the fabric using tailor's chalk, keeping them parallel to the cut bias edge.

Cut out the strips and sew them together to produce the required length of piping. Fold the piping, right way out, around the cord. Use a zipper foot on your sewing machine to stitch along the seam allowance close to the cord.

If the piping is intended to go all the way around the object, you will need to join the ends. Unpick the stitches at one end of the fabric strip and trim the cord so the two ends butt together. Fold under the top raw edge of fabric and stitch the join together.

Piping should be inserted into the seam as you stitch the main seamline. With right sides of fabric facing, insert the piping strip matching the raw edges. Stitch it in place using a zipper foot.

Flat Piping

This is made in the same way as covered piping, but the cord is omitted.

Bias binding *figs 31 and 32*

Bias binding can be bought ready made, or you can make your own. To make, cut bias strips measuring four times the required finished width. Press the binding in half lengthways with wrong sides together, then press under the raw edges so they almost meet at the crease.

To apply the binding, fold it over the raw edge of fabric and pin, then top stitch it in place through all the thicknesses. When turning corners, fold the binding diagonally to form a mitre.

Alternatively, open out the binding and, with right sides together, stitch one edge of the binding to the edge of the fabric. Fold the binding to the wrong side and slip-stitch it in place over the line of machine stitching.

fig 30a Cutting bias strips

fig 30b Joining strips

fig 30c Covering cord

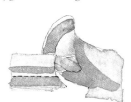

fig 30d Joining ends

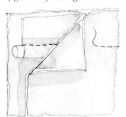

fig 30e Inserting in seam

▲ *Covered piping adds a distinctive edge to a seam. You can make your own by cutting and joining strips of bias-cut fabric and wrapping this around a length of cord. The raw ends of fabric can be finished neatly when the piping is inserted into the main seam at construction stage (above).*

Braids, ribbons and fringing *fig 33*

There are hundreds of different kinds of braids and ribbons from delicate ric rac to heavy bullion fringing. Whichever you use, be sure that the trimming suits its purpose and enhances the object rather than disguising it. The colour of a trimming should either match the object perfectly or be in complete contrast. Braids, ribbons and fringing are generally top stitched in place by machine or sewn by hand, taking care to stitch it close to the edges. Velvet ribbons should be sewn in place using a zipper foot to avoid crushing the pile.

Gathered frills *fig 34*

A frilled edge can add a soft and pretty finishing touch. A frill can either be single, made from one thickness of fabric, or double which eliminates the need for a hem and produces a full and luxurious look.

To make a double frill, cut twice the required depth adding double the seam allowance. Fold the frill in two with the fabric the right way out and the raw edges matching. Gather the top by sewing two rows of machine stitches on the longest setting just above the seam allowance. Gather up the fabric as required.

Lace

Lace can add a pretty finishing touch to bedding, cushions and sheer curtains. It should be top stitched in place over a narrow machine stitched hem turned to the right side of the fabric. If the lace has an unfinished edge, it can be seamed into the fabric using a narrow 6mm (1/4in) seam allowance. Press the seam upwards and oversew the edges for a neat finish.

Buttons and beads

Buttons and beads can be used to highlight a specific area on an item. Tab-headed curtains can be given a button detail, a throw looks splendid with a beaded fringe and a simple cushion can be transformed into a work of art with buttons sewn on in a decorative pattern. There are no rules when it comes to what you use and where, but you should make sure that the practical use of an object is not compromised by the decoration. For safety's sake, items trimmed with buttons and beads should be kept out of the reach of small children.

Appliqué *fig 35*

Appliqué is the technique of stitching a patch of fabric to an item to make a decorative feature, with the stitching becoming a part of the design. You can make up your own designs or you can cut patterns from ready printed fabric. Appliqué can be done by hand but it is quicker and easier to use a machine, which gives a neat, durable finish.

To machine appliqué, roughly cut out the shape to be applied. Tack the patch in place just outside the outline of the motif, then stitch around the outline using a small straight stitch. With a closely-spaced zigzag stitch, sew over any lines which form part of the pattern inside the motif. Zigzag over the stitched outline. Cut away the excess fabric close to the stitching, using embroidery scissors.

A fast, effective method of appliqué is to use double-sided stiffening fabric which simply bonds the neat-cut shape to the fabric before sewing. This eliminates the awkward stage of cutting around the appliquéd shape and the stiffening fabric also prevents the edges from fraying.

Embroidery *figs 36 and 37*

Embroidery adds delicate detail to all kinds of home furnishings and can transform even the plainest piece of cotton. Embroidery is easy but it requires patience, as a good effect depends on neat, even stitching.

You can buy embroidery transfers which are simply ironed onto the fabric, leaving a faint outline which can be embroidered over. You can also trace your own motifs from books or from other fabrics. Threads are available in various thicknesses so choose one to suit your project.

The most commonly used embroidery is satin stitch which is used for filling in or shading an area. Outlines can be created with running stitch, backstitch, chain stitch or lazy daisy stitch.

fig 31 Top stitched bias binding

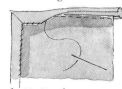

fig 32 Hand-sewn bias binding

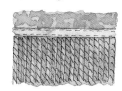

fig 33 Fringing

fig 34 Gathered frills

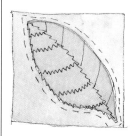

fig 35 Appliqué

fig 36 Satin stitch

fig 37 Lazy daisy stitch

1·6 FASTENINGS AND FIXINGS

Fastenings are generally used on items which need to be removed regularly for cleaning, such as duvet, cushion and loose upholstered covers. Fastenings may also be added as decorative trims on all kinds of home furnishing projects.

The general rule when using a fastening is to choose one which is appropriate to the weight and type of fabric.

You may find the thought of inserting a zip or making a buttonhole daunting but neither is difficult and, where an opening needs to be firmly and neatly fastened, these may be the most practical solutions.

Zips

Zips are available in a variety of sizes, weights and colours. It is important to choose the correct weight zip for the fabric you are using and you will find this information on the packet. Try to match the colour of a zip as closely as possible to your fabric to make it unobtrusive unless, of course, it is to be a decorative feature.

Inserting a zip in a seam *figs 37 and 38*

Measure the length of the zip opening from the tab to the bottom of the teeth. Mark the length of the zip, plus an additional 5mm (¼in), in the middle of the seam. Stitch the rest of the seam, right sides facing, leaving the opening for the zip. Tack the edges of the opening together to prevent the fabric from slipping, then press the seam open.

Place the open zip face down over the centre of the seam. Pin and tack one side of the zip in place. Stitch along the edge of the tape, 3mm (⅛in) away from the zip teeth. Close the zip. Pin and tack the other side of the zip in position. Turn the fabric the right way out and, using a zipper foot, stitch all around the zip just outside your tacking.

Offsetting a zip *fig 39*

A zip can be completely concealed in a seam and this is known as offsetting the zip. Mark the length of the zip onto your seam and stitch the seam, leaving the opening for the zip as described above. Open the zip

and place it face down over the opening so the teeth are in line with the middle of the right-hand seam allowance rather than over the seam. Pin and tack one side of the tape in position. Close the zip and tack the remaining side through the other seam allowance. On the right side of the fabric, stitch as close as possible to the ends of the zip using a zipper foot.

Inserting a zip in a piped seam *fig 40*

The piping should be attached to one side of the seam without sewing closed the opening. Place the open zip face down on the piped seam so that the teeth are in line with the piping stitching. Tack and sew the zip in place, stitching 3mm (⅛in) away from the teeth. Turn back the seam allowance so that the piping lies at the edge of the opening. Close the zip.

Press under the seam allowance of the other piece of main fabric and bring the folded edge over the zip so that it meets the piping. Tack the seam through all thicknesses and machine stitch 6mm (¼in) from the folded edge and across the ends of the zip up to the piping.

Buttons *fig 41*

Buttons need to be sewn on firmly as it can be difficult to find an exact match should you lose one. Determine the position of the button and secure the thread at this point on the right side of the fabric. Slide the button over the needle down to the fabric.

To make even stitches, place a matchstick or toothpick over the top of the button and work the stitches over it. When you have finished, remove the matchstick and pull the button up so that the slack threads are below. Wind the working thread around the slack several times to make a shank for the button. Fasten off the thread into the shank.

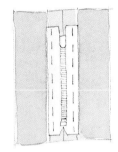

fig 37 Inserting a zip in a central seam

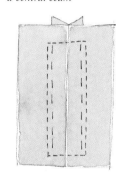

fig 38 Stitching the zip in place

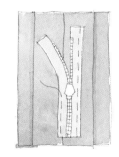

fig 39 Offsetting a zip

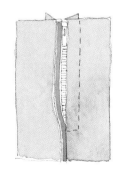

fig 40 Inserting a zip in a piped seam

Buttonholes *fig 42*

To make a hand-worked buttonhole, draw the width and position of the opening onto your fabric, using tailor's chalk. Decide on the depth of the stitched edge and draw this allowance around the opening to make a rectangle; 2-4mm ($^1/_{16}$-$^1/_8$in) gives a standard-sized edge. Sew a line of running stitches around the rectangle. Carefully snip along the opening line to each end of the rectangle, then oversew the raw edges (see page 16).

To strengthen and neaten the raw edges, work around them using buttonhole stitch. Insert your needle into the edge of the buttonhole with the needle pointing away from the opening. Loop the thread around the back and underneath the needle. Pull the needle through and out of the fabric to complete the stitch, pushing the resulting knot to the top of the needle so that it sits on the edge of the buttonhole. Continue around the buttonhole, keeping the stitches uniform in size and close together.

Looped buttonholes *figs 43 and 44*

Decorative looped buttonholes are ideal for cushions or covers and are made from a narrow strip of bias-cut fabric. This is seamed and turned the right way out using the end of a blunt tapestry needle.

The end of the strip or rouleau, should be pinned in position on the right side of the fabric with all the raw edges matching. Make the strip into loops for the buttons, leaving approximately 1cm ($^2/_3$in) between loops. Tack and stitch the loops just inside the seam line before attaching a facing.

Press fasteners *fig 45*

Press fasteners are made either from metal or plastic and are available in various sizes. The fastening consists of two halves which snap together with a ball and socket. Each side of the fastener has small holes which enable you to stitch them to the fabric.

To apply a fastener, mark its position on the fabric and separate the two halves; the ball half should be positioned on the overlapping fabric and the curved socket on the underlap.

Position the top half of the fastener on the fabric approximately 6mm ($^1/_4$in) from the edge. Secure the thread underneath and stitch through the holes one at a time until they are firmly attached, taking the needle under the fastener to the next hole. Finish off the thread. Sew the opposite side of the fastener in position in the same way.

As an alternative to individual fasteners, it is possible to buy plastic press fasteners attached to an integral fabric strip which can be sewn along both sides of the fabric.

Press stud fasteners or poppers

These come in two halves and are fixed in position on either side of the fabric. They are attached using a special tool which is available from most department stores.

Fastening tape

This touch-and-close tape is ideal for fastening duvet covers and joining large pieces of fabric. It is available in strips or as small pads. The tape has two halves; one with small plastic loops and the other with a felted surface. The two lock firmly when pressed together but can be easily separated and re-sealed time after time. The opposing sides of the tape should be stitched or stuck to the corresponding edges of fabric.

Ties

Ties are ideal for fastening cushions and covers. They can be made from narrow, bias-cut strips of fabric, ribbon or binding and are stitched into the seam.

No-sew fastenings

Adhesives and staple guns can be used for many projects. Adhesives are ideal for making lampshades or attaching trimmings and finishing touches, so long as you use a suitable one for your materials. A glue gun is a worthwhile purchase as the glue sticks on impact and is easy and accurate to apply.

Staple guns are available from DIY and hardware stores and come in different weights for lightweight to heavy duty usage. Use them for instant furnishings to fix fabric to a curtain pole, to put up a shelf liner or to staple fabric to a screen.

fig 41 Creating a shank for a button

fig 42 Hand-sewing a buttonhole

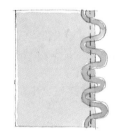

fig 43 Attaching looped buttonholes

fig 44 Looped buttonholes

fig 45 Press fasteners

2

LIVING ROOMS

All rooms can be transformed by attractive furnishings, but because comfort is such a priority in a living room, you can make the most of the more luxurious fabrics available. From furniture covers to cushions, and curtains to lampshades, this room offers ample opportunity for you to express your own sense of style in creating a unique look.

You may opt for the clean, uncluttered lines of a contemporary look, using woven fabrics in natural colours. Alternatively, a more traditional feel can be achieved using rich velvets and damasks finished with heavy bullion fringing and tassels.

When selecting fabric for a living room, take inspiration from the main colour areas already in the room such as floor coverings, upholstery and wallpaper. Choose fabrics which will co-ordinate with these to create a harmonious balance between patterns and plains.

2·1 CHAIR THROW

A throw is a length of fabric which is draped over a chair or sofa to make an easy, informal covering. Throws can be simple, adding a touch of elegance, or sumptuous with decorative details such as luxurious braiding, buttons or beads.

A throw is a wonderfully easy way to add a creative touch to a plain chair or sofa and can also be used as a clever disguise for a shabby piece of furniture which has seen better days. Easy to make, a throw is simply a large square or rectangle of fabric which is hemmed on all sides.

Measuring fabric

There are no hard and fast rules about how large a throw should be, but you do need to take into account the size of the object you wish to cover and the effect you wish to achieve. You may want to cover the entire thing, as in the case of a tatty sofa, or simply to add a decorative panel of fabric.

Choosing fabric

For a traditional look, it is worth investing in a good quality, weighty fabric which drapes well. If you favour a more contemporary look, a light woven cotton is more suitable.

It is important to consider a few basic practicalities when choosing your fabric. The material should be crease-resistant, easy to wash and should not show dirt easily. You may like to leave the edges of the throw plain or add a decorative finish, such as the chenille bullion fringe and small beads that have been sewn to the ends of the throw pictured here.

Making a basic throw

First measure your chair or sofa. If your throw is to cover it completely, include extra fabric for tucking around the seat pads and to allow it to drape to the ground on all sides. Cut your material to the right size, joining widths of fabric if necessary. Turn over, press and stitch a narrow double hem on all four sides of the fabric. If the fabric is bulky, you may need to mitre the

corners of the throw to finish them neatly (see page 18).

Sew a length of braiding either to the top or underside of the throw, depending on whether you wish the upper edge of the braid to show. The fringing can either be machine stitched in place over the narrow hem or may be hemmed into place by hand. Turn under a narrow raw edge at each end for a neat finish. Hand stitch small, co-ordinating buttons at regular intervals along the top of the fringing.

POINTS TO CONSIDER

■ If you have a selection of mismatched furniture, you can also make matching fitted covers for chairs to co-ordinate with your throw.

■ A two-layered throw has a stylish, decorative look. A large throw made from plain fabric is used to cover the furniture and a smaller throw in a patterned fabric is arranged on top.

▼ *A throw may be smaller than the object it covers, adding a decorative touch. If it is larger, it can be tucked neatly over the pads, retaining the outline of the piece of furniture (below).*

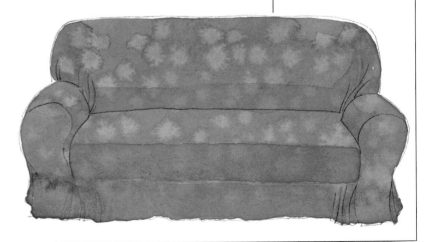

2·2 BASIC CUSHION COVERS

Cushions are an ideal way to add instant colour and style to a room. They can be made in a variety of shapes, sizes and fabrics and the finished cushions can be as plain or as decorative as you wish.

The most basic cushion is made by sewing together two pieces of material with wadding sandwiched between. However, cushion covers give a professional finish and can be removed easily for washing.

Square cushion covers

To make a square cushion cover, measure the cushion pad to make a pattern for the top piece (see page 14). For the back piece, cut two rectangles by dividing the area of the cushion pad in half widthways, adding a 1.5cm (1/2in) seam allowance on each piece.

Pin the pattern pieces to the fabric, making sure that any fabric patterning is central. Cut out the three pieces.

Constructing the cushion

Place the two rectangles of the back piece together with right sides facing. Tack and stitch each end of one long seam leaving a central opening for the zip. Press the seam allowance open and pin the zip into the opening covering the zip teeth. Use a zipper foot on your sewing machine to stitch the zip in place as close to the teeth as possible.

Press the seam allowances and open the zip. Place the back and the top piece together, right sides facing. Pin, tack and sew around the edge and then clip the corners to minimise bulk. Turn the cover the right way out and insert the cushion.

Round cushions

Measure your cushion (see page 14) and cut out two main pieces and a gusset.

Cut the gusset in two, one piece being 3cm (1¼in) longer than the zip. Cut this piece in two lengthways. Place the two halves together, right sides facing and sew a short seam at either end of one long side to create a central opening for the zip. Press open the seams and sew in the zip.

Trim 3cm (1¼in) from the long side of the remaining piece of gusset and seam the short ends of the gusset pieces together to form a hoop, leaving 1.5cm (1/2in) unstitched at end of each seam. Press the seams open.

With right sides of fabric facing, pin, tack and sew one circle to one edge of the gusset, matching the raw edges. Open the zipper and then attach the second circle in the same way, matching the fabric grain on both circles.

Press the seams toward the gusset and clip notches into the seam allowances so they lie flat. Turn the cover the right way out and insert the cushion.

Bolster cushions

Measure and cut a rectangle of fabric for the bolster body (see page 14). Fold it right sides together and stitch the end of each seam to make a zip opening. Sew in the zip and open it. Join a circle of fabric to each end of the tube and clip notches around the circular seams to ensure they lie flat. Turn the bolster cover the right way out.

POINTS TO CONSIDER

■ Cushions can be made from all kinds of fabrics from hard-wearing, washables to luxurious silks and velvets.

■ Make a selection of cushions in co-ordinating colours or match them to curtains and other home furnishings.

■ Circular cushions may be made flat using the same method as a square cushion, but the addition of a gusset gives a much sturdier end result and a more professional finish.

▼ *The zip on a circular cushion should be inserted into the centre of a section of the gusset piece. The remainder of the gusset fabric is then joined to either end of this section (below).*

2·3 DECORATIVE CUSHIONS

Cushions use a relatively small amount of fabric so you can afford to use more extravagant fabrics and trimmings. Luxurious looking cushions will give a sumptuous lift to the plainest of living rooms.

The basic structure of a trimmed cushion is the same as that of a plain cushion, with trimmings such as fringing, beading and tassels added when the cover is complete. However, if you wish to add piping along the main seams it is best to do this when sewing the seams together.

Appropriate decorations
There are a wide variety of trimmings available with which to decorate cushions. Piping, braid and fringing can be used to embellish the seams, whereas buttons, beading or decorative fabric panels can be added as surface decoration to the main fabric area.

Piped cushion with tassel trim
The cream cushion here has been piped with a matching cream fabric to give an elegant, classic look. It is trimmed with a large tassel of the same colour at each corner. The piping is sewn into the main seams of the cover when the front and back of the cushion are joined (see page 20). A tassel is then hand-sewn to each corner once the cushion cover has been turned the right way out.

Insertion cord trim
A particularly useful way to add a decorative edge to a cushion whilst it is being made is to use insertion cord. Insertion cord is a length of cord attached to a bias strip of fabric. The cord can be sewn into the seams of the cushion cover when the two halves are joined in much the same way as standard piping.

Fringed cushion
A length of fringing can be sewn around a plain cushion within the seam or added to the cushion cover when it is complete.

Measure the length of fringing required to fit all the way around the cushion and then add a little extra to allow you to finish the ends neatly.

Either stitch the fringing onto the edge of the completed cushion cover or insert it into the seam and sew it in place at construction stage, butting the edge of the fringing against the raw edges of fabric.

For a neat finish, fold under the raw edges of the trimming at each corner and neatly stitch them into place.

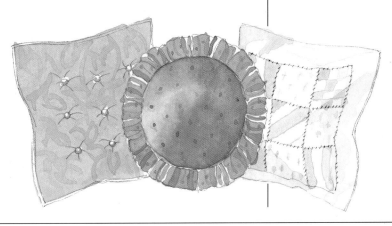

POINTS TO CONSIDER

■ Co-ordinate the colour of trimmings with the main fabric for a classic look or team complimentary colours with bright, plain fabrics for a contemporary feel.

■ First and foremost a cushion should always be functional. Take care when positioning buttons and beads that they do not hinder comfort.

▼ *As well as piping, fringing and tassels, there are other means of adding a decorative finish to cushions. A row of stylish buttons, a frill, or a patchwork panel can all add interest (below).*

2·4 LINED CURTAINS

Many people are wary of making lined curtains, especially for large windows. However, the techniques involved are the same as for simpler projects and, so long as you measure up correctly and can stitch a straight seam, curtains are easy.

There are two advantages to choosing lined curtains over the unlined variety. A lining can add a full sumptuousness, giving a luxurious look which is particularly suited to large windows. In addition, the lining protects the main curtain fabric from the effects of strong sunlight and damp from the window surface, increasing the life span of the curtains.

Creating a suitable work environment
When working with large amounts of fabric, you must ensure that you have a suitably large, flat work surface. If you do not have a big enough table, you can spread your fabric out on a clean floor and use this as your work area. Before you begin, you should make sure that your fabric is flat and free of creases.

If your windows are large, you will probably need to join widths of fabric to achieve the required measurements. In this case, take care to match any patterning to ensure a professional finish.

Measuring fabric
Fix your chosen track on the wall above the window, positioning the track or pole to flatter the window (see page 12).

Measure the required depth from the track to the floor, adding the required seam and hem allowances.

The width of your curtains is dependent on the chosen heading. Once you have decided on the style of heading tape, calculate the width measurement accordingly (see page 19), adding extra for seam allowances.

Cutting the fabric
Double check your measurements before you cut any fabric then cut as many fabric widths as you need, cutting out both the

main curtain fabric and the lining fabric. Join the widths as necessary with right sides of fabric facing, using a 1.5cm (½in) seam allowance and matching any patterning across the seams. When making a pair of curtains, ensure that the pattern matches across the two when they are closed.

Press the seams open and make snips into the seam allowance up to the stitching at 15cm (6in) intervals along the length of the curtain; this will prevent the seams from puckering. Join the widths of lining fabric in the same way.

Mitring corners
Turn and press a single 5cm (2in) hem on both side edges of each curtain, then turn and press a single 10cm (4in) hem along the bottom edge. Insert a pin on each hem piece at the point where the two raw edges of fabric meet. Unfold the hems.

Fold over the corner of fabric between each pair of pins and press it flat. Re-fold the hems over the turned-in corners to complete the mitres. Hand sew a curtain weight into each corner hem if required.

▼ *Mitring the corners on the hems of curtains gives a neat, professional finish. These are easily created by inserting a pin marker on the edge of each adjacent hem at the point where the two meet (fig 1). The hems are then unfolded and the corner of fabric between the pins pressed over (fig 2). The bottom hem is then re-folded, encasing the corner fabric (fig 3) and the side hem re-folded to create a neat diagonal join (fig 4).*

fig 1 *Marking the hems*

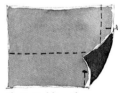

fig 2 *Folding the corner*

fig 3 *Re-folding the hems*

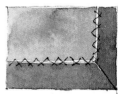

fig 4 *Completed mitre*

Stitching the hems

Herring-bone stitch the hems all around the curtain and slip-stitch along the diagonals at the mitred corners.

Attaching the lining

Lay the main fabric flat with the lining on top, wrong sides facing. Ensure that the lining is positioned centrally over the main fabric, then pin the curtain fabric and lining together with a row of pins running down the centre.

Turn back one side of the lining and lock stitch the two fabrics together, finishing just above the hem (see page 17). Smooth the lining down over the curtain, turning back a second fold, parallel to the first and 40cm

Applying a heading

Treating the two fabrics as one, press over 5cm (2in) along the top edge. Cut a length of heading tape to the same width as your curtain, adding a little extra for turning under. Tack the heading tape to the top of the curtain, 6mm ($\frac{1}{4}$in) down from the top edge, tucking under the raw ends of the tape at each side.

Knot the cords on the tape together at each end. Stitch the tape in place around all four sides. Slip curtain hooks into the heading tape approximately 13cm (5in) apart and pull up the tape from the outside edge of the curtain to fit the track. Ease the curtain fabric along the cords to create uniform gathers.

◁ *The curtain fabric and the lining should be cut and sewn at the same time. The completed lining is then attached to the curtain by means of columns of lock stitch (left).*

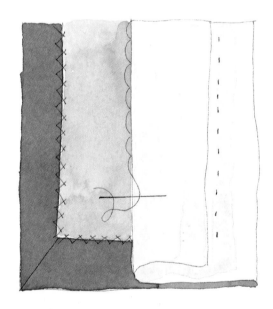

(16in) apart. Lock stitch along this fold. Working on either side of the centre line, toward the outer edges of the curtain, lock stitch the two fabrics together with vertical rows of stitching approximately 40cm (16in) apart.

Finishing the edges

Carefully trim down the lining to match the outer edges of the curtain. Turn under 2.5cm (1in) on the side edges and 5cm (2in) on the bottom edge of the lining, forming neat corners and press. Slip-stitch the lining to the curtain down the sides and along the bottom edge with small, neat stitches.

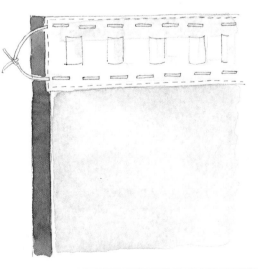

◁ *When the lining is in place, the top of the curtain can be turned over and the heading tape stitched in place. The curtains are then gathered and the ends of the cord tied with a secure knot (left).*

2·5 CLASSIC TIEBACKS

As well as keeping curtains away from the window glass, tiebacks are an ideal way to add a shaped frame to a window and to create a decorative finishing touch to co-ordinate with your curtains.

Tiebacks can be ornamental as in the case of embellished brass hold-backs or sumptuous tassels, or as classically simple as a plain band of fabric. Although they are generally made from the same fabric as the curtains, there are no hard and fast rules so use your imagination to create your own designer masterpieces from all kinds of fabrics and furnishing accessories.

Measuring fabric
Whatever the shape and style of tieback you choose, you need to take time to position the tiebacks at the correct height on the wall, taking into account the proportions of the window.

Generally, they should be positioned two thirds of the way down the curtain, but this will depend on the shape of the window and the effect you wish to create.

To obtain the required length of your tieback, hold a tape measure loosely around the curtain at the required height, adding 3cm (1¹/4in) for seam allowances.

Crescent tieback
The most conventional style of tieback is the crescent tieback. Its curved shape is practical as it causes minimum creasing to the curtains.

Drawing a template
To make a piped crescent tieback, you should first make a paper template. Draw a rectangle half the length of the required tieback and approximately 11cm (4¹/2in) wide. Gently curve both sides of the strip so that one end is narrowed down to about 4cm (1¹/2in). Cut out the pattern.

Fold your fabric in half. Lay the template on the fabric with the wide end of the template against the fold. Cut two pieces of fabric for each tieback.

Sewing the fabric
A heavyweight, iron-on interfacing is used to stiffen the tiebacks. Use the template to cut one piece of interfacing, omitting the seam allowances, and apply it to the wrong side of one of the fabric pieces.

Attach piping or insertion cord to one fabric piece (see page 20) then, with right sides facing, stitch the tieback pieces together, leaving an opening for turning through. Trim the seams and clip the curves. Turn the tieback the right way out and slip-stitch the opening. Neatly sew a curtain ring to each end of the crescent.

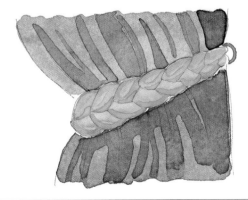

POINTS TO CONSIDER

■ Buy fabric for both curtains and tiebacks at the same time to ensure a perfect colour match.

■ The tiebacks do not have to be made from matching fabric. The use of a contrasting fabric can create a stunning, contemporary look.

■ A more luxurious look can be achieved by adding sumptuous piping or tassel trimming to the edge of the tiebacks.

◀ *Alternative classic tiebacks can be made by simply plaiting three tubes of fabric together. Lightly pad the fabric with a little wadding to give a plump, professional finish (left).*

2·6 TABLE LAMPSHADES

It is not always easy to find the perfect lampshade to co-ordinate with your furnishings or to suit a particular shape and size of lamp base. By making your own, you have the freedom to choose every element of the design.

To support the shade you will need two lampshade rings: a plain one for the base and one with a gimbal fitting (an inner ring on two arms) for the top. These rings are available from department stores.

Making a template
The first step in making a lampshade is to make a card template. Draw a large inverted 'T' shape on a piece of card and mark the diameter of the bottom lampshade ring centrally on the horizontal line.

Measuring from the horizontal line, mark the required height of the lampshade on the vertical line. At this height, draw a second horizontal line the same length as the diameter of the top lampshade ring.

Using a ruler, draw diagonal lines joining the ends of the diameter lengths from the bottom line to the top line. Continue the lines until they cross the central vertical to form a triangle.

Drawing a curve
Attach a pencil to one end of a length of string and a drawing pin to the other. Press the pin into the top of the triangle and adjust the length of the string to draw an arc which passes through both corners at the base of the triangle.

Keeping the pin in position, adjust the string to draw a second arc which passes through the points where the upper horizontal line meets the diagonals.

Cut out the template, wrap it around the lampshade rings and mark the overlap. Draw a line 2cm (³/4in) beyond the overlap and cut away any excess card.

Making a lampshade
Lay the card template onto a sheet of fire-retardant PVC backing material. Draw around the template and cut this out. Peel

off the backing paper and gently smooth the backing onto the wrong side of your fabric. Cut around the backing, leaving enough excess material to turn over. Cut notches into this material at regular intervals and turn it over, gluing or taping it in place.

Constructing the shape
Fold the stiffened fabric round to form the lampshade shape and peg it in position around the top and bottom rings. Mark the overlap seam using a pencil and remove the pegs. Glue the overlap and leave it to dry. Apply glue around the top and bottom of the shade and insert the rings, holding them in place with pegs while the glue dries.

Finishing touches
Finish the top and bottom edges of the lampshade with bias binding or braiding to cover the rings. If you want your lampshade to be plain, cover the rings with self-adhesive binding tape before gluing them in position.

POINTS TO CONSIDER

■ The size of your lampshade is determined by the size of the lampshade rings and its shape defined by the difference in size between the lower and upper rings; the bigger the difference, the wider the resulting lampshade will be.

■ For safety's sake, homemade lampshades should always be used with bulbs of 60 watts or less and should never be used with a naked candle flame.

■ Once you have mastered the basic techniques, you can experiment by adding trimmings, ribbons and other finishings or use paint techniques to make one-off designer pieces.

▼ *When making your own lampshades, you need to begin by drawing a template onto card. The size of your lampshade rings will determine the dimensions of your template (below).*

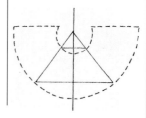

2·7 PLEATED WALL SHADES

These pretty pleated shades are simple to make yet look effective and can be made to co-ordinate with other furnishings in the room. You can use almost any fabric but should treat it with a spray or paint-on retardant to ensure that it is safe.

Pleated wall shades can be made using remnants of fabric. You could use leftover fabric from a pair of curtains to continue a particular theme or choose fabric which matches a dining room tablecloth or chair covers. Alternatively, you can use wallpaper or cardboard as the basic shade material.

Whether you use fabric, paper or card, this type of lampshade is only suitable for use with low wattage bulbs of 40 watts or less and should never be used with a naked candle flame.

Measuring and cutting fabric

To make the shade, cut a strip of fabric measuring approximately 130cm (52in) by the required depth of the finished shade; 12cm (4³/4in) is an ideal depth for a wall shade of this type.

Stiffen the fabric using either a spray-on starch or a self-adhesive backing, following the manufacturer's instructions. Check beforehand that the product you intend to use is flame-retardant.

Pleating the fabric

On the wrong side of the fabric, draw vertical lines across the width at 4cm (1¹/2in) intervals, then fold backward and forward along these lines to create a concertina effect.

Working on the right side of the fabric, use a single hole punch to make a hole in each pleat 1cm (¹/4in) down from the top edge and 1cm (¹/4in) in from the outer fold of the pleat. On the reverse side, punch a second set of holes 3cm (1¹/4in) from the top and 1cm (¹/4in) from the outer fold of the pleats. Use scissors to snip from the folded edge to each hole in this lower row to enable you to insert the lampshade ring.

Overlap the two ends of the fabric to create a tube and glue the overlap in place.

When the glue is dry, thread a length of narrow ribbon through the top set of holes, spacing the pleats evenly. Slip the ring into the lower holes and adjust the ribbon to create the desired lampshade shape. Secure the pleats in place by tying the ribbon in a neat bow.

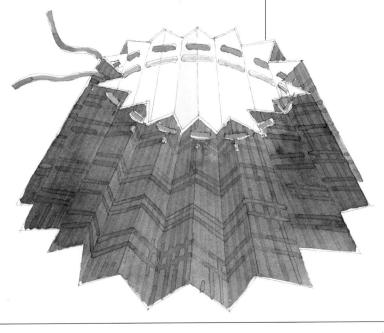

POINTS TO CONSIDER

■ These shades can be made from fabric left over from larger projects or bought remnants which makes them cost-effective.

■ Your room will probably need other light sources as shades of this size are only suitable for use with low wattage light bulbs.

■ Pretty ribbon or cord can be added for a decorative effect.

■ Use natural fabric decorated with dried flowers and leaves for a contemporary look.

▼ *A decorative ribbon trim pulls the pleated fabric into the desired lampshade shape. (below).*

2·8 PICTURE FRAMES

These easy to make fabric picture frames are a wonderful way to use up small scraps of fabric to make co-ordinating accessories for your home. The basic frame shape is cut from card and softly padded with wadding.

To make a basic rectangular picture frame, cut two pieces of thick cardboard approximately 6cm (2¹/₂in) larger than the size of the picture you wish to display. Cut a piece of paper the same size as your picture and position this in the centre of one piece of card. Draw around the paper template and cut out the rectangle to make a window in the frame.

To make the frame spacers, cut two pieces of thin card 5cm (2in) shorter and 1cm (¹/₄in) narrower than your main frame pieces. Lay one spacer piece centrally on the frame front piece, lining the two pieces up along the base edge only. Mark the frame window onto the spacer and cut it out.

To make the stand, cut a piece of card approximately 12cm x 4cm (4³/₄in x 1¹/₂in). Make a mark 2cm (³/₄in) from the bottom edge on each side of the card. Draw a line from each of these marks to the centre of the base of the card to form a point. Cut out the stand.

Covering the frame

Using the frame front piece as a template, cut out a piece of wadding the same size and shape. Cut a piece of fabric slightly larger than the card and lay the fabric wrong side up onto a flat surface.

Lay the wadding in the centre of the fabric and place the card front piece on top. Stretch the raw edges of fabric up and over onto the cardboard backing and glue them in place; glue the two long sides first and then the shorter sides to achieve an even finish. You can use masking tape to hold the fabric in place while the glue dries.

Cut out the rectangular centre, leaving enough fabric to turn back. Stretch the fabric onto the back of the frame and glue it in place, clipping into the corners to minimise any bulk and make a neat finish.

Cut pieces of fabric to cover the remaining rectangle of thick card and the stand and glue them in place, trimming and tucking under all the raw edges of fabric to give a neat finish.

Assembling the pieces

Glue the blank rectangular spacer centrally to the inside of the frame back, matching up the base edges only. Glue the windowed spacer to the back of the frame front in the same way and allow the glue to dry.

Glue the frame front and back pieces together, applying fabric adhesive all around the frame edge. Use clothes pegs to hold the pieces of the frame together while the glue is drying.

Line up the base of the stand with the frame and mark the position of the top of the stand on the back of the frame. Sew the stand to the back of the frame using small, neat stitches.

To protect your photographs and pictures, cut a piece of clear acetate to fit the frame opening and sandwich it between the spacers.

POINTS TO CONSIDER

■ Fabrics with a small repeat pattern are most suitable for use as a project of this size can easily be overpowered by a large pattern.

■ The frame may be made to any shape or size following the same basic method.

▼ *The front and back sections of the frame are separated by card spacers which are glued into position after all the pieces have been covered with fabric (below).*

2·9 COVERED FOOTSTOOL

Although most furniture is generally upholstered with fixed covers, loose covers can be used to create a whole new look for old furniture or to co-ordinate mismatched pieces. They also have the added advantage of being easily removed for laundering.

The cover on this footstool is made from one square of fabric to which a decorative piped frill is added. The fabric is then simply slipped over the footstool to make a practical loose cover.

Measuring fabric

Measure the footstool across the width and length of the pad to estimate the size of the main cover piece. The fitted part of the cover should extend to the depth of the pad and the frill should hang loosely down to disguise the legs of the stool.

Making the basic cover

For the fitted cover, cut a piece of fabric to size allowing a 1.5cm (¹/2in) seam allowance all the way around. Lay the fabric centrally over the footstool, wrong side up. Pin along the corners of the stool smoothing the fabric along the stool sides for a smooth, even fit. Trim away the excess triangle of material at each corner, leaving a 1.5cm (¹/2in) seam allowance. Remove the cover from the stool and stitch the seams.

Measure around the circumference of the stool and make up enough covered piping to fit around the edge of the cover. Using a zipper foot on your sewing machine, stitch the piping in place (see page 20).

Adding the frilled edge

Cut a strip of fabric measuring twice the circumference of the stool and twice the desired length of the frill, adding a 1.5cm (¹/2in) seam allowance all around. Stitch the short edges of the strip, right sides facing, to form a loop and press the seam open. Fold the strip in half widthways, wrong sides together. Using the longest machine stitch, sew along the seam allowance near the raw edge through both thicknesses of fabric. Leave the ends of the threads long.

Pull the threads to gather up the frill and pin the fabric around the bottom edge of the cover with right sides facing and raw edges matching. Distribute the fullness of the fabric evenly around the edge of the cover and, using a zipper foot on your sewing machine, stitch the frill in place. Trim and finish the seams neatly.

POINTS TO CONSIDER

■ Choose a hard-wearing fabric which co-ordinates with curtains, cushions or other home furnishings.

■ When pinning the top piece of fabric over the stool pad, work across diagonal corners to keep the grain of the fabric straight and ensure a smooth, tight fit.

■ To create a contemporary look, use plain fabric piped in a contrasting colour and finish the cover with a straight, fitted skirt.

▼ *The top piece of the footstool cover is created from a single rectangle of fabric which is seamed at the corners. When measuring the fabric, take the length in each direction from the base of the cushion pad on one side across to the base of the opposite side (below).*

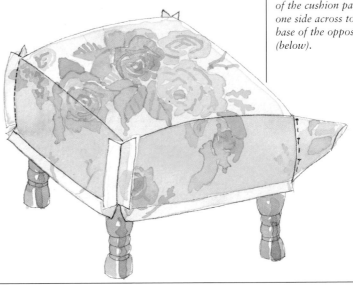

3

DINING ROOMS

The versatile nature of fabric decor really comes into its own in a dining room. Tablecloths, napkins, place-mats and chair covers can all be used to change the feel and look of a room to suit specific occasions. A set of table linen made from practical, washable cotton for everyday use can be replaced with an opulent table setting in a more luxurious fabric such as linen or damask on special occasions.

Fabric can add richness and depth to a dining room and can also be used to transform and disguise mismatched furniture with the addition of stylish covers. A simple tie-on cushion or fitted slip-over cover can instantly elevate a junk shop chair into a stylish seat. Walls and windows can also benefit from a touch of splendour, provided by wall hangings and curtains with sophisticated headings.

3·1 RECTANGULAR TABLECLOTH

Quick and easy to make, a square or rectangular tablecloth is simply a hemmed piece of fabric which can be elegantly plain or opulently lavish with decorative trims. Corner pleats can be added to give a smart, fitted appearance.

Standard square or rectangular cloths for small tables can be made from just one width of fabric, but tablecloths for wide tables will usually require you to join widths. When joining fabric, you should ensure that the seam does not lie centrally on the finished cloth and that you match patterns exactly.

Joining fabric widths

Cut the pieces of fabric to the required length and width, allowing a little extra for pattern matching; one piece should serve as the central panel whilst the other should be cut in half lengthways. Pin and tack the half widths to the sides of the central panels and seam the pieces together.

Making the basic tablecloth

Measure your table to calculate the amount of fabric required (see page 14). Cut out the necessary fabric widths and seam them together with a flat fell seam, giving a neat finish with two rows of stitching showing on the right side (see page 17).

Hem all four bottom edges of the cloth; you can simply hem each side but, for a neat, professional finish, you should mitre the corners (see page 18).

Adding trimmings and finishings

Once you have mastered the art of making a basic tablecloth, you can then experiment with decorative details such as fringing and frills. A fitted cloth with neat piped edges has an elegant look which is suitable for both everyday use and special occasions.

Cutting a fitted tablecloth

Cut a piece of fabric the same dimensions as your tabletop with added seam allowances. Cut one rectangular panel to fit each of the four sides of the table; the width

of each should be the same width as the table side and the length cut to the required drop. Add seam allowances to all the pieces.

Making pleats

To make a pleat, cut a square of fabric with each side measuring the same as the the drop of your tablecloth, with added seam allowances on all sides. Draw a gentle curve from one corner to its opposite, add a seam allowance and cut out the fan-shaped piece of fabric. Cut a further three pieces of fabric in the same way.

Assembling the pieces

Press and stitch a narrow double hem along the rounded edge of each of the pleat pieces and the bottom edge of each side panel. Sew covered piping all around the tabletop piece, joining the ends neatly (see page 18). Stitch covered piping to both straight edges of each pleat piece. Sew the table side panels together to form a loop, inserting a pleat piece in each corner. Pin and stitch the loop to the tabletop pieces, sandwiching the piping in the seam.

POINTS TO CONSIDER

■ For informal table settings, choose plain or printed cottons which are machine washable. For special occasions, there is nothing more dramatic than a crisply laundered linen cloth to provide a background for sparkling glassware and cutlery.

■ When buying fabric for a tablecloth, consider buying extra to make co-ordinating napkins.

■ Although a tablecloth will provide some resistance to heat from hot plates and mugs, you should always use a table liner (a piece of thick, heat-resistant fabric) to prevent scorch marks and white heat marks on a wooden table.

▼ *Curved inserts of fabric are added to each corner of a fitted tablecloth. These fall into neat pleats, giving a stylish, elegant look (below).*

3·2 ROUND TABLECLOTH

As the main focal point in a dining room, a well-dressed table can radically transform the room, adding style or evoking mood. Beautifully polished tabletops will also benefit from being covered by a cloth to prevent scratches and heat marks.

Fabric for your tablecloth can be chosen to co-ordinate with curtains and other fabric furnishings in the room, and a luxurious feel can be achieved by adding piping, frills or even a tasselled trimming. However, whichever style you choose, you must consider what the table is to be used for. A tablecloth for family meals will need to be hard-wearing and washable, whereas a covering for special occasions will warrant a more luxurious, extravagant fabric.

Cutting the basic cloth

To make the basic cloth, measure your table (see page 14) and decide on a suitable diameter which gives the desired drop. You should take into account any additional length that you intend to add, for instance a frill or contrasting border. Add a hem allowance and cut a square of fabric to this measurement. You may need to join widths of fabric to achieve your full measurement and, in this case, you should cut a central panel using the full width of the fabric then add a strip of fabric along each side, joining the selvedges. Press any seams open.

Shaping the cloth

To create the circular shape, you will need to make a makeshift compass using a length of string, a pin and a tailor's chalk pencil. The pencil and pin should be tied at opposite ends of the string with the length between them equal to half your diameter measurement. Fold the fabric into four and pin around the edges. Lay the fabric on a flat surface and press the pin of your compass into the folded corner. Draw an arc on the cloth.

Pin the layers of fabric together just inside the arc then cut through all the layers to produce a round piece of cloth.

Make up enough covered piping to fit the

circumference of the cloth and stitch it to the right side of the fabric, raw edges matching (see page 20).

Adding the frill

To make the frill, cut a fabric strip $1^{1/2}$ times the circumference of the cloth and twice the depth you require, adding seam allowances. You may have to join several widths of fabric together to achieve the circumference measurement.

Seam the strips, right sides facing, to form a loop and press the seams flat. Turn the fabric the right way out and fold the frill in two, bringing the raw edges up to meet. Press it flat. Run a line of gathering stitches along the seam allowance at the top edge of the fabric and pull the fabric into gathers to fit the edge of the tablecloth.

With right sides of fabric facing, pin the frill to the tablecloth, sandwiching the piping in the seam (see page 20). Stitch all the pieces together in one go, using a zipper foot on your sewing machine. Trim back the seams and neatly finish any raw edges (see page 17).

POINTS TO CONSIDER

■ You can experiment with layers of colour to co-ordinate with china and tableware, or mix patterns, textures and shapes; a circular base cloth will look effective if used with a square over cloth in contrasting fabric.

■ For special occasion cloths, you can add your own finishing touches. Choose trimmings which suit the style of the room and complement your table setting.

▼ *The shape of a round tablecloth is achieved by drawing an arc on the folded fabric using a makeshift compass made from a tailor's chalk pencil, a drawing pin and a length of string (below).*

3·3 EMBROIDERED NAPKINS

Although napkins are not expensive to buy unless you opt for the finest linen or lace, by making your own you can add decorative details giving your napkins a truly personal touch.

Plain napkins are ideal for every day use and, as they require so little fabric, they can be made from remnants in just minutes. Hard-wearing, washable fabrics such as cotton, cotton mix or linen are the most practical choices as your napkins will need to be laundered on a hot wash, time and time again.

Plain napkins also allow you the opportunity to add creative touches such as bound edges, cutwork appliqué or embroidery. Alternatively, you can stencil or stamp on your own colours and patterns using fabric paints.

Making a basic napkin
Before you start, you should determine the size you wish the finished napkin to be; a 45cm (18in) square is a good basic size. Press the fabric and cut out as many napkins as you require, adding a 3cm (1¼in) seam allowance all around each one. Press and stitch a 1.5cm (½in) double hem on all four sides, mitring the corners to give a neat finish (see page 18).

Adding embroidered corners
Machine embroidery adds an elegant and personalized touch to napkins and linens, and many machines have a selection of embroidery programmes.

Delicate stitching in all one colour gives a fresh look, whereas using thread the same colour as the fabric gives a sophisticated, self-patterned finish.

The embroidery can trim the edges or be contained in just one or all four corners. If you intend to embroider corners, it is best to do so before hemming the edges. You may find that once the corners are complete that you wish to continue the embroidery along the sides. You can draw up your own designs, working them out on paper before

transferring the shapes to the fabric using tailor's chalk. Alternatively, you can use one of the embroidery transfers available from all good haberdasher's. By using a transfer, you can ensure an even and professional-looking motif.

Creating the embroidery
Carefully position the transfer in one corner of the napkin and iron it so that the ink leaves a faint outline on the fabric. Hand or machine embroider over the outline with small neat stitches (see page 21).

Shaped edges
To shape the napkin edge, draw your chosen shape onto the fabric using tailor's chalk. To ensure the pattern matches on all four sides, fold the napkin into four and press. Cut the required shape into all four thicknesses of fabric at the same time and then unfold the fabric and press it flat.

Set your sewing machine to a wide, close satin stitch and work your way around the edge of the napkin, following the shaped outline to create a neat finish.

POINTS TO CONSIDER

■ Save all your fabric scraps and offcuts to make a medley of napkins for general use.

■ Personalizing napkins with initials or a simple motif gives an elegant touch for family meals or special occasions.

■ Potato prints applied using fabric paints provide children with the opportunity to create their own masterpieces.

■ A set of napkins with delicate, embroidered patterning makes a beautiful gift.

▼ *An alternative decorative finish can be achieved by binding the napkin edges with contrasting fabric (see page 21). The corners can be mitred (see page 18), creating a neat and professional finish (below).*

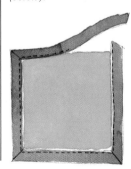

3·4 UNLINED CURTAINS

As opposed to the solid formality and grandeur of heavy lined curtains, unlined curtains provide a translucent finish to windows, allowing some light in but still providing privacy.

A variety of heading tapes can be used with unlined curtains, yet one of the simplest, effective headings is the tab heading which has plain, shaped or decorated loops of fabric at the top of the curtains which slot straight onto a pole.

Measuring and cutting curtain fabric

Measure the required width and drop of your curtains (see page 12); 1-1½ times is an ideal width, as too much fabric causes gathers and the tab effect will be lost. The drop of the curtain should be measured from just above the window recess.

Cut the fabric for your curtains, adding an extra 10cm (4in) for the hem and 5cm (2in) for side turnings. Add a 3cm (¼in) seam allowance to any widths of fabric you need to join and join them with a flat fell seam (see page 17). Cut a facing for the top of each curtain, measuring the same width as your curtain and 9cm (3½in) deep.

Making tabs

To make each tab, cut a 30cm x 20cm (12in x 8in) rectangle of fabric; on check fabric, cut across the diagonal for a decorative finish. Fold the fabric in half lengthways, right sides together, and seam the long edge. Fold the tab in half again lengthways and cut a diagonal from one end, approximately 3cm (1¼in) along the folded side to the end corner of the seamed side.

Unfold and press the tab so the seam runs down the centre of one side and the cut end forms a point. Stitch around the pointed end then turn the fabric right way out.

Cover buttons with matching fabric and stitch one to the pointed end of each tab.

Constructing the curtains

Stitch double narrow hems on the sides of the curtain pieces and stitch a double 5cm

(2in) hem at the bottom, mitring the corners (see page 18). Stitch narrow double hems on both short sides and one long side of the facing. With right sides together, pin the facing to the top of the curtain, sandwiching the raw ends of the tabs at regular intervals in between. Seam along the top, then turn the right way out. Fold the pointed ends of the tabs over to the right side of the curtain and slip-stitch them in position.

POINTS TO CONSIDER

■ Unlined curtains are generally made from lightweight fabrics which should be pre-washed to prevent any shrinkage.

■ There are no hard and fast rules concerning the amount of tabs you need. It is best to make too many and pin them in position to see how the fabric falls.

■ Extra insulation can be given to lightweight curtains during winter, by making detachable linings which hook onto the track behind the curtains.

▼ *A pretty alternative to tab heads is to sew pairs of ties between the facing and curtain which can be tied into bows on the curtain pole (below).*

3·5 CLIP TOP CURTAINS

A simple yet stylish method of hanging curtains is to use curtain clips. These metal clips grip the fabric and are simply slotted over the curtain pole, requiring no heading tape or special headings.

Curtain clips have become very fashionable in recent years and are one of the simplest ways to hang curtains. The clips have a spring mechanism which holds the top of the curtain fabric firmly, and keeps it in place on a curtain pole. The finished effect is perfect simplicity and ideal for contemporary settings.

Suitable fabrics

Curtain clips are not suitable for use with thick, heavy fabrics as the grip is invariably not strong enough to hold the weight. Check that the clips can hold the weight of your fabric before making up and hemming your curtains.

Measuring the fabric

Measure the required drop of your curtains (see page 12) and add 16cm (6¹/₂in) for the top and bottom hems. For the width of the fabric, you will first need to decide how full you want the curtains to be. The fullness is dependent on how far apart you space the clips. Widely-spaced clips create large, loose folds and you will need 1¹/₂-2 times the width of fabric. Clips positioned closely together will require only 1-1¹/₂ times the window width of fabric. An additional 6cm (2¹/₂in) should be added for side seams.

Hemming the curtains

Press and stitch 3cm (1¹/₄in) double hems at the side seams. Press over a 4cm (1¹/₂in) double hem at the top and stitch it in place. Top stitch the hem by machine or slip-stitch it by hand. Hem the bottom of the curtain in the same way.

Hanging the curtain

Fix the curtain clips to the top of the curtain and slip them over the curtain pole. Arrange the clips, to achieve the desired

draped effect, ensuring that the spaces in between are even.

Alternative ways of hanging curtains

There is a multitude of inventive ways of hanging curtains without using headings. One of the simplest is to punch a row of metal eyelets along the hemmed top of the fabric. The curtains can then be suspended from a pole in a number of ways using cord, fabric ties or curtain rings. Another alternative is to fix a length of curtain wire with tension fittings into a window recess. The curtains are threaded onto the wire, which is then tightened using the tension fittings so that the curtains hang properly.

POINTS TO CONSIDER

■ A clip-headed curtain looks particularly effective if draped to one side of the window.

■ Clips are ideal for hanging sheer curtains as the fabric can be bunched up under the clip and draped in layers.

■ Clips are available in a host of designs ranging from plain to highly decorative and can also be used in conjunction with tasselled cord to make elegant tiebacks.

▼ *For a contemporary look, clip the top of the curtain with bulldog clips. The curtain can then be suspended from a tension wire which is threaded through the holes in the tops of the clips (below).*

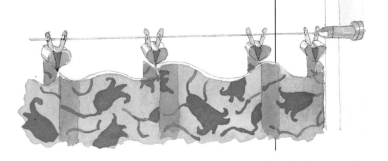

3·6 CREATIVE TIEBACKS

Curtain tiebacks do not have to adhere to the formal fabric band design. With a little imagination, there is a whole host of materials which can be adapted to hold your curtains in place, whilst creating an individual look.

The most basic tieback is a length of braid, cord or fabric which ties around the curtain and is secured with a bow or knot. This is simply undone when you wish to draw the curtains and re-tied when the curtains are pulled back. The cord is threaded through a loop on the wall which pulls the curtain clear of the window.

Simple cords

The ends of a simple tieback can be finished to give a more ornate look. Adding tasselled ends to a silky cord creates a classic look, whereas wide strips of organza can be tied into striking glamorous bows which work particularly well with a voile curtain.

Which materials?

Any material that is sufficiently flexible to wrap around the curtain and tie into a knot can be used, but be sure to pick a material which suits the weight and style of your curtains. Pretty printed silk scarves work well with light, sheer bedroom curtains, whereas a rustic twine laced with dried herbs and flowers is more suited to a country-style kitchen.

Thick rope can be loosely bound around the fabric and then tied in a decorative knot to create a nautical look. This can then be decorated with shells, starfish and other objects found on the beach which fit the theme. Sections of old fishing net also make a good base for a nautical tieback.

Fixed tiebacks

Once you have selected your material, you can add surface decoration. If your tieback is purely decorative and is not going to be untied and re-tied to release the curtain, you can really go to town, gluing and threading through a wide range of decorative elements. Experiment with shells, flowers,

small kitchen accessories such as antique cutlery and petit fours moulds or objects trouvés. Almost anything can be used in this decorative fashion, simply threading it through the loops of the tieback cord, tying it with thin cords or gluing it into position.

Functional decorations

If the curtains are not fixed and are in regular use, the decoration needs to be easily removed. In this case the elements can be suspended on thin cords, leading to a single hook which can simply be lifted off the binding cord.

POINTS TO CONSIDER

■ When gluing decorations to tiebacks you must be sure that the glue is strong enough to hold the weight of the objects over an extended time period. A hot glue gun gives a strong bond and has the added advantage of sticking the required items instantly.

■ For functional tiebacks, the decorative elements can be glued together to form a single solid shape and a hook attached to the back. Add a hardboard backing where the objects are irregularly shaped and difficult to join to one another.

▼ *A whole host of materials can be used to decorate a basic tieback. Decorative beads add a touch of Bohemian class, silk scarves are effective with sheer curtains, dried fruits, chilli peppers and herbs add a rustic touch to kitchen curtains and even a plug and chain can look effective (below).*

3·7 SLIP-OVER CHAIR COVER

An ordinary chair can be given a luxurious upholstered look with the addition of a slip-over cover. It is a wonderful way to co-ordinate mismatched furniture or to disguise a drab individual piece.

Using plain fabric, you can make the cover in just two pieces. The main piece fits from the front of the chair seat, across the seat pad and over the backrest to the floor. The second piece fits around the chair as a skirt.

Measuring and cutting the fabric
Measure your chair and cut out your fabric pieces (see page 15). Make up covered piping to fit around the front of the chair from back strut to back strut (see page 20).

Fitting the cover
Lay the main fabric piece over the chair seat and back with the right side of the fabric facing the chair, allowing 1.5cm (¹/₂in) to hang over the front edge of the seat. Pin the fabric together down the sides of the backrest, then pin a narrow hem around the back skirt. Mark the position of the edge of the seat on the fabric, using tailor's chalk. Snip away the surplus fabric at the corners.

Sewing the main piece
Remove the cover and trim off the excess fabric around the chalk line, leaving a 1.5cm (¹/₂in) seam allowance. Stitch the side seams from the top of the chair to the seat and then hem the remaining back skirt. Replace the cover on the chair.

Making the frilled skirt
Stitch a narrow double hem along three sides of the skirt piece. Stitch two parallel rows of gathering threads along the remaining long side, approximately 1.5cm (¹/₂in) and 2cm (³/₄in) from the raw edge.

Adding piping
Pin the piping around the seat from one back strut to the other. Gather the skirt and pin this to the seat, sandwiching the piping between the two layers of fabric. Remove

the cover from the chair and tack and stitch the skirt in place.

Making ties
To make the ties, cut and sew four 50cm (20in) lengths of narrow binding cut on the bias of the fabric (see page 20). Hand stitch one tie on either side of opening at the back of the chair.

POINTS TO CONSIDER

■ Use fabric which is both hard-wearing and washable. Dark patterned fabrics are ideal for chairs which are in everyday use.

■ If you are using a patterned fabric, you will need to seam along the top of the chair so the pattern runs the right way up on both sides of the backrest.

■ A frilled skirt gives a soft, feminine finish; a smart, contemporary look can be achieved with a straight skirt and contrasting piping.

▼ *The chair cover is made in two pieces with the main piece covering the seat pad, backrest and forming the back skirt and the second piece creating a frilled skirt around the remaining three sides (below).*

3·8 WALL HANGING

Decorative wall hangings have been a popular addition to many homes since medieval times. Embroideries or tapestries were often pictorial references to recent events, but even a plain hanging can add colour and warmth to a bare wall.

The size and style of your wall hanging is entirely a personal choice, but you should remember to keep the finished article in proportion to the room. Large, bold hangings look striking in a spacious room yet, in a small room, such a hanging would be claustrophobic.

You also need to consider where you intend to position it. If it is to be hang above a chair, you need to take into account the height of the chair when measuring up.

A dramatic look can be achieved by suspending a pair of hangings from a curtain pole either side of a central fireplace, window or piece of furniture.

Cutting the fabric

When you have decided on the finished size of your hanging, cut out two rectangles of fabric, adding 8cm (3in) to the top for the heading and a 1.5cm (½in) seam allowance on the other three sides. Place the fabric right sides facing, fold it in half lengthways and press. Measure approximately 25cm (10in) from the bottom of the folded side and mark this point with a pin (this measurement should be adjusted to suit the size of the finished hanging). Cut a straight, diagonal line from the pin to the opposite bottom corner. Open up the fabric to reveal a pennant shape and press it flat.

Constructing the pennant

Pin the two main pieces together with right sides of fabric facing and stitch around the sides and the bottom, using the seam allowance. Snip away the corners of excess fabric at the bottom points and snip into the seam at the central 'V'. Trim the seams, turn the fabric right way out and press it.

You can either sew piping into the seam whilst joining the fabric or sew it onto the outside of the pennant afterwards.

Attaching piping

Tasselled tiebacks make a pretty decorative edging as the tassels are already attached to a long length of co-ordinating piping. However, you can use ordinary piping and stitch on separate tassels once you have sewn the piping in place.

Pin the piping around the outside edge of the pennant, arranging it so that the tassels fall at the bottom points. Unpick a couple of stitches in the seam at the 'V' of the pennant and tuck the ends of the trimming into the gap. Slip-stitch the opening closed, securing the piping in place. Stitch the trimming around the outside of the pennant by hand, using small, neat stitches.

Making the heading

Press under 1cm (¼in) to the wrong side of the fabric along the top edge of the pennant and then press under a further 7cm (3in) to create a casing (you may need to adjust the size of the casing to fit the diameter of your curtain pole). Pin and stitch the fabric in place and then thread the hanging onto your curtain pole.

POINTS TO CONSIDER

■ Use heavyweight fabric which hangs well to create a wall hanging for a dining room or formal setting.

■ Embroider or appliqué motifs onto the fabric for a personalized touch to complement your decor.

■ Alternative headings will create different looks. Other options include tabs, ties or eyelets.

▼ *The classic pennant shape is easy to cut by folding the fabric pieces in half and cutting off one corner. When applying the piping, it is best to start at the centre of the 'V' (below).*

4
KITCHENS

In a functional room such as a kitchen, your main consideration should be that the furnishings are practical. There is no point in having elaborate swags and tails at windows, or tablecloths which drape theatrically to the floor which will not only get in the way, but may also cause a fire hazard.

The furnishings here are likely to become soiled easily and so it is important to choose washable fabrics which do not show marks easily. Patterned fabrics are ideal in this respect and can give a co-ordinated look to a room. You should also aim to keep as much natural light in the kitchen as possible, opting for plain curtains or blinds which provide privacy but still let in the light.

Finishing touches are what really make a difference in the kitchen. A tablecloth and matching place-mats will brighten up the breakfast table, and remnants of fabric can be used to make shelf liners or cover jam pots for a rustic look.

4·1 PRETTY CAFÉ CURTAIN

This pretty half curtain is ideal for a kitchen as it provides privacy whilst allowing light into the room. Alone, it has a simple, classic look, yet it can also be teamed with a matching valance, giving a soft frame to the top of the window.

Café curtains are best made from a washable cotton or sheer fabric which is sufficiently lightweight to hang from a net rod or café pole; suitable fittings can be bought from department stores or fabric shops. Light colours let in the most light and have a delicate, airy look, but strong colours should not be ruled out as they can look striking.

A café curtain can be fitted inside the window recess or fixed to the wall either side of it. Hold the fabric up against the window beforehand to see which best suits your room.

A curtain inside the recess looks neat and is practical for a kitchen window above a sink. A curtain outside the recess looks best if teamed with an attractive net rod and can be used to make a small window look wider or longer.

Choosing a fitting
Choose a café pole which compliments both your fabric and the surroundings. Plain wooden poles evoke a rustic country cottage feel, whereas striking wrought iron designs work well with gothic surroundings and light sheer fabrics. A brass pole is a smart option which blends well with many styles.

Measuring the fabric
Measure your window to gauge the required width and depth of your curtain. Multiply the width of the window 1¹/2-2 times depending on the fullness required for the finished curtain. Add 2.5cm (1in) for each side seam allowance and 12cm (4³/4in) for the top and bottom hems.

Hemming the curtain
Turn a double 1cm (¹/2in) hem to the wrong side of the fabric along each side seam. Stitch this into place by machine or slip-

stitch it by hand. Turn and press 1cm (¹/2in) of fabric along the top edge of the curtain then turn under a further 5cm (2in). Press and pin this into place. Sew along this fold, 5mm (¹/4in) from the edge to form a casing (you should adjust the size of the casing to suit the size of your curtain rod).

Turn and press 1cm (¹/2in) along the bottom edge and turn over a further 5cm (2in) to create a hem. Slip-stitch the hem in place. Thread the curtain onto the pole and adjust the gathers.

POINTS TO CONSIDER

■ For a contemporary look, exchange the traditional pole for a length of ribbon or rope. This can be threaded through large eyelets punched into the top of the curtain.

■ Plain sheer café curtains can be printed using fabric paints to give an individual look.

■ Decorative trimmings or edgings can add a luxurious look to a simple curtain.

▼ *As an alternative to a gathered curtain, make a scalloped heading using a saucer as a template for the scallops. Thread the curtain onto the pole using decorative rings attached to the scallops (below).*

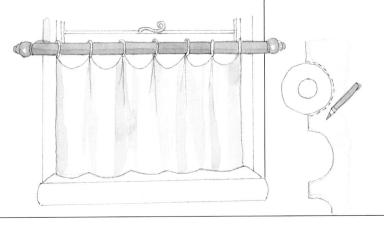

4·2 BORDERED TABLECLOTH

This two-fabric approach has a contemporary look and is an ideal way of using up remnants of co-ordinating fabric. The double thickness of the border adds weight to the edge of the cloth which helps the fabric to drape elegantly.

The addition of a pretty border offers a simple alternative to a plain tablecloth and it can be made from plain or patterned fabric in contrast to the main cloth. When measuring the main fabric piece, it is important to remember that the border will add depth to the drop of the tablecloth and you should allow for this accordingly.

Cutting the main fabric piece
Measure your table to calculate how much fabric you will need to make the main piece (see page 14). The panel should be long enough to hang over the sides of your table with a drop of 25cm (10in), plus a 1.5cm (1/2in) seam allowance all the way round. Cut out a central panel from the main fabric, joining widths of fabric if necessary.

Cutting out the border
To make the contrasting border, cut four strips of fabric each measuring twice the required depth plus seam allowance. The strips should be the same length as the sides of your central panel with an added allowance for mitring. The mitring allowance should be equal to the depth of the border strips and should be added to each length of the border strips. If you are using a patterned fabric, you may need to add extra fabric to allow you to match patterning at the seams.

Sewing the border
Fold each of the border strips in half lengthways with the right sides of fabric together and press.

To mitre each corner, draw a 45° angle from the bottom folded edge to the the top raw edge, using a tailor's chalk pencil. Lay the strips out flat and pin two strips together, right sides facing, along the lines you have drawn.

Using the 1cm (1/4in) seam allowance, pin, tack and stitch along the seam and then snip off the point of excess fabric at the corner. Mitre all the corners in the same way and then turn the fabric the right way out. Press the border, matching the mitred seams on the front and back layers of the fabric to create neat corners.

Attaching the border
With right sides of fabric facing, pin, tack and sew one edge of the border to the raw edge of the main panel. Press the seams toward the border, then turn in the seam allowance on the raw edge of the border and oversew it by hand along the seam line.

POINTS TO CONSIDER

■ Ensure that the two fabrics are of the same weight for a neat, professional finish.

■ You can add piping in between the border and the central panel for a luxurious look.

■ For a tablecloth designed for everyday use, chose practical, washable cotton or cotton mix fabrics.

■ As an alternative to a straight border, scallop the hem using a cup or saucer as a template.

▼ *Mitred corners give a neat and professional finish and are created by sewing a 45° pointed seam between two sections of the double-depth border. The end point of fabric should be cut away to minimize bulk (below).*

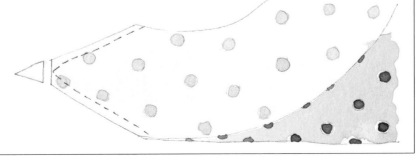

4.3 QUILTED PLACE-MAT

Place-mats add a decorative feel to a table, especially if matched to napkins and other soft furnishings. The softly quilted style has a practical application in that it protects the table when using hot plates and serving dishes.

These place-mats are easy to make by sandwiching a piece of lightweight wadding between two layers of decorative cotton fabric. The quilting is best done using a sewing machine and the design can be as simple or as elaborate as you wish.

Measuring and cutting the fabric

To decide on the right size for your place-mats, measure the diameter of a dinner plate and add a little extra fabric to this measurement to create a border. For a complete place setting, a rectangle of fabric measuring 45cm x 30cm (18in x 12in) is an ideal size. Cut two rectangles of fabric and a piece of wadding to the chosen size for each mat, adding a 1.5cm (½in) seam allowance. Cut and make up enough piping from contrasting fabric to fit around the outside of the mat (see page 20). Pin the three layers together and, using a saucer as a template, cut rounded corners into the mat.

Sewing the basic shape

Place one piece of fabric on top of the piece of wadding, with the right side of the fabric uppermost, and stitch contrasting piping all around the mat, butting and joining the ends neatly. Lay the remaining fabric piece on top, wrong side uppermost, sandwiching the piping between the two layers of material. Stitch all the way around the mat, leaving a small opening at the lower edge for turning through. Carefully trim the excess material from around the seams and turn the mat the right way out. Turn the raw edges in and neatly slip-stitch the opening closed.

Quilting

Using tailor's chalk and a ruler, draw a parallel line all the way around the perimeter of the place-mat. The line should

be approximately 4cm (1½in) in from the piping and should follow the curved corners of the place-mat.

Carefully sew along the chalked line using a medium length machine stitch to make the first line of quilting. Then, using the edge of the machine foot as a width guide, carefully stitch a second line 5mm (¼in) further in from the first to complete the quilted effect.

POINTS TO CONSIDER

▓ Choose fabric which can be mixed and matched with your table wear and linen for a smart, co-ordinated look.

▓ If making a set of place-mats, buy sufficient material to make the required number of place settings plus extra mats for serving dishes.

▓ Place-mats don't have to be quilted, piped or shaped. To add instant style to your table, simply hem rectangles of heavy cotton fabric in lush, bright colours or subdued natural tones.

▼ *The piping and wadding of this simple place-mat are sewn into place on one piece of fabric. The second piece of fabric is then sewn into position, encasing the piping in the seam (below).*

4·4 FITTED CHAIR CUSHION

Whilst being a practical choice for kitchens and dining rooms, wooden chairs are not always the most comfortable of seating arrangements. Padded chair cushions can add extra comfort and give a welcoming feel to the room.

These cushions are designed to fit the shape of the seat and are kept in place with pretty ties which fit around the posts of the backrest. In this way the cushion remains firmly in place on the seat whilst in use, but can be easily removed for cleaning.

Measuring and cutting the fabric
Measure the seat size and shape to make a pattern (see page 15). Cut out the fabric for the seat cover and frill, marking the position of the leg struts. Cut and make up sufficient piping to fit around the seat cushion (see page 20).

Adding the piping
Starting and finishing at the centre back of the cover, tack the piping around the edge of the top cover piece, with right sides of fabric facing. Snip the turnings so that the piping fits around the corners.

Stitch the piping into place using a zipper foot on your sewing machine. Finish the piping neatly by folding under the raw ends and stitching them in place (see page 20).

Making the ties
Cut two strips of fabric measuring 1m x 13cm (40in x 5in). Fold each piece in half lengthways with right sides together. Hem all the way round using a narrow 5mm (1/4in) seam allowance and leaving a central opening for turning through. Turn the fabric the right way out and slip-stitch the opening. Fold each tie in half and tack it to the position marked on the top piece.

Attaching the frill
Press and sew a 7mm (1/4in) double hem along the two short sides and one long side of each frill piece. Gather stitch the remaining raw edge of the frill and pull up the gathers to fit around the top cover.

With right sides facing and raw edges matching, tack the frill to the top cover, enclosing the piping.

With right sides facing, sew the two cover pieces together with a 1.5cm (3/4in) seam allowance, using a zipper foot on your sewing machine. Leave the back section open for turning through. Trim the seams and snip into the curves before turning the cover the right way out.

Using the seat pattern, cut out a piece of wadding and trim a small amount from around the outside edge. Fit the pad into the cover and slip-stitch the gap closed.

POINTS TO CONSIDER

■ For practical use, choose dark colours and patterns which do not show dirt easily.

■ Your chosen fabric should be hard-wearing, but easily washable.

■ Frilled cushion covers look charming in a rustic-style kitchen. An alternative contemporary look can be achieved by adding a gusset in place of the frill. For this style you will need to make up twice the quantity of piping to position round both the top and bottom of the gusset section.

▼ *The piping and frill on this chair cushion are fitted into the seam for a neat finish. The piping is stitched in place around one of the main pieces and then the frill is tacked on top. All the pieces are then sewn together in one go when the second main piece is added (below).*

4·5 ROLLER BLIND

A roller blind is one of the simplest window dressings and its clean, unobtrusive lines make it suitable for most settings. A co-ordinated pelmet which hides the mechanism at the top of the blind gives a neat and attractive finish.

A roller blind can be made to fit a window recess or can extend beyond the window's perimeter to make the window look larger. Although you can construct the blind mechanism yourself, it is easier to use a shop-bought blind kit which contains all the parts that you need.

Measuring fabric for the blind
Calculate the required dimensions of the blind (see page 13) and deduct 1.5cm (¹/2in) from the width on either side to allow for the mechanism. Add 20cm (8in) to the drop to allow for the casing and covering the roller. Cut out the fabric and apply a fabric stiffener following the manufacturer's instructions. The raw edges of the fabric should not need hemming as the stiffener prevents fraying.

Making up the blind
Cut the roller and lath to the required width. Make a 4cm (1¹/2in) double hem at the bottom of the blind and stitch it close to the edge to form a casing. Insert the trimmed lath and stitch the openings closed.

Turn 1.5cm (¹/2in) of the top edge of the blind to the right side and tack this to the roller. Fix the pulley mechanism in position and slot the blind into the brackets.

Fitting a pelmet shelf
A self-adhesive card pelmet can be cut to size, covered with fabric then attached to a pelmet shelf which fits above the window.

Calculate the size of your pelmet (see page 19) and fix the pelmet shelf above the window. If your blind is recessed, the shelf should be just wider than the architrave. If the blind is fixed to the wall, the shelf should be 5cm (2in) wider at each end. It should be no more than 5cm (2in) deep to avoid interfering with the blind mechanism.

Making the pelmet
The basic structure of a pelmet is cut from one piece of card which fits along the front of the pelmet shelf and folds back on either side to completely encase the shelf. The bottom edge of the pelmet can be left straight or cut to create a patterned edge.

Measure around the pelmet shelf and cut a piece of double-sided, self-adhesive card to fit. Shape the bottom edge if required.

Applying a fabric finish
Cut a piece of fabric just larger than the card. Remove one side of the backing from the card and smooth the fabric onto the surface. Remove the second backing and fold over the raw edges of fabric, snipping the curves to prevent puckering.

Cut a piece of lining for the backing, adding 1.5cm (¹/2in) all round for turning under. Line the back of the pelmet, turning under the raw edges and slip-stitching them into place. Fold the ends of the pelmet back to make side panels. Fix self-adhesive tape to the back of the pelmet and the top of the pelmet shelf. Fix the pelmet in position.

POINTS TO CONSIDER

■ Roller blinds are best suited to small windows. To dress a large window, it is better to use two or three blinds in co-ordinating fabric to create the effect of one large blind.

■ Self-adhesive black out material can be used to line the blind to give a dense, opaque finish at night.

■ On a large window where the pelmet is heavy, secure the pelmet to the shelf at the corners using small tacks to prevent it from slipping.

■ Be inventive and create your own designer pelmet. You can shape the edges with curves, triangles, zigzags – in fact, any shape that can be cut into the edge.

▼ *A fabric pelmet is easy to attach to a pelmet shelf and is a neat and attractive way to cover the mechanism of the blind (below).*

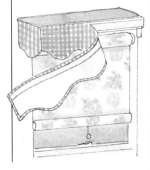

4·6 FABRIC-LINED CUPBOARD

Give an old cupboard a new lease of life by adding a smart fabric curtain to the front panel. Fabric panels are an ideal way of pulling a collection of mismatched furniture together to create a co-ordinated look for your kitchen.

The curtain for this cupboard has a narrow cased heading and is threaded onto curtain wires which are fixed to the inside of the cupboard door at the top and bottom of the open panel.

Preparing the cupboard
A huge variety of attractive secondhand cupboards can be found in junk shops and car boot sales for a fraction of the cost of new furniture. With just a little effort, you can transform an old panelled cabinet into a stylish and desirable piece of furniture.

Prepare the surface of the cupboard before you paint it. Remove any old paint first and then sand the wood to a smooth finish. Knock the front panel out of the cupboard door and smooth any rough edges with sandpaper. Prime the wood before applying an undercoat, then paint the cupboard and allow it to dry thoroughly before fitting the curtain wires and fabric.

Measuring the fabric
To calculate the size of the curtain, measure the length of the opening in the cupboard door and add a further 10cm (4in) to allow for top and bottom casings. Measure the width of the opening, then multiply this measurement 1½-2 times, depending on how full you want the gathers to be.

Making the curtain
Turn over and stitch narrow double hems down the sides of the curtain. Turn over and pin a double 2.5cm (1in) hem at the top and bottom of the fabric. Stitch along the edges of the turnings to make narrow casings to carry the curtain wires.

Cut two pieces of curtain wire to fit the width of the top and bottom of the cupboard panel. Screw an eye into each end of the curtain wires. Thread one length of

wire through the top casing and the second through the bottom casing.

Fitting the curtain
On the back of the cupboard door, mark the position for each pair of screw hooks to support the curtain wires. A screw hook should be fitted either side of the panel near the top and bottom of the door.

Attach the curtain wire eyes to the screw hooks to hang the curtain in position. Distribute the gathers of the curtain fabric evenly across the panel opening.

▼ *A rustic country look can be achieved by adding a chicken wire or mesh panel to the front of the cupboard before lining it with fabric (below).*

4·7 PADDED NOTICE-BOARD

A pretty fabric-covered notice-board is an ideal way to use up remnants and provides a functional area for displaying cards, recipes and general memos. Choose a bold, fun fabric or one which co-ordinates with other fabrics in the room.

This notice-board has a chipboard base and is covered with a soft layer of wadding. The crisscross pattern of braid is kept in position with upholstery studs and forms a mesh to keeps papers safely in place.

Cutting the board

First you should decide on a suitable size for your board; bear in mind that the chipboard base can make a large notice-board heavy which may be unsuitable for hanging on some walls. A board measuring 46cm (18in) square, cut from 12mm (1/2in) thick chipboard gives sufficient space without being too weighty. Use a coping saw to cut rounded corners and smooth any rough edges with fine sandpaper.

Applying the fabric covering

Lay the board on a sheet of lightweight wadding, draw around it and cut out the wadding shape. Draw around the board onto the wrong side of your fabric, ensuring that any patterning is central. Add a 5cm (2in) allowance all the way around and cut out the fabric.

Lay the fabric shape wrong side up on a flat surface. Position the wadding centrally and lay the chipboard on top. Pull the fabric excess up onto the back of the board at each corner. Smooth out any creases in the fabric and staple it in place at the corners.

Working your way around the sides, pull the fabric taut over the board and staple it in place. Keep the fabric as smooth as possible, taking care not to pull it too hard which will stretch the material. When you have finished stapling, cut away any bulky excess fabric.

Attaching the braid

Stretch a length of gimp or braid diagonally across the board. Staple the ends in place on

the back of the board, pulling the length taut. Cut away any excess braid. Continue to fix all the braids to the board in this way, keeping the lengths straight and the spaces between them equal.

Using a hammer, knock in an upholstery stud at each point where two braids cross. Place a scrap of wood between the hammer and the stud to prevent the head of the stud from denting or spoiling.

Applying the backing

Lay the board face up on a piece of lining fabric and draw around it, adding 5mm (1/4in) for turning under. Cut out the shape. Press a turning of 1cm (1/2in) to the wrong side of the lining and lay the fabric centrally on the back of the board. Neatly staple the lining to the board.

Hanging the board

Fix a pair of picture rings approximately 14cm (51/2in) down from the top edge of the board and 5cm (2in) in from the outside edges. Thread through a length of picture wire and tie it securely in place.

▼ *The same method can be used to create a whole host of useful wall hanging ideas. A smaller board, piped with cord and punctuated with cup hooks makes an ideal holder for keys (below).*

4·8 ROMAN BLIND

This stylish blind is backed by lines of parallel tape which allow the fabric to hang straight or be drawn up into neat horizontal pleats. It is economical on fabric, yet gives a luxurious feel to a window.

Before making your blind, you must first decide whether you wish it to hang in the window recess or flat against the wall. This type of blind needs to be fitted to a pelmet board, batten or special track so, wherever it is positioned, you must ensure that there is enough room for a line of screw eyes to be inserted between the front of the blind and the wall, but not so much that the blind hangs away from the window.

Measuring and hemming the fabric
Holding the batten in position, measure the required drop of the blind and add 11cm (4¹/2in) for top and bottom turnings. Measure the width of the blind and add 4cm (1¹/2in) for side hems. Cut a piece of fabric to size and turn, press and stitch 1cm (¹/4in) double side hems. Turn the top of the fabric under 1cm (¹/4in), then a further 4cm (1¹/2in) and stitch it into place.

Fitting the tapes
Mark vertical sections across the blind, 25cm-30cm (10in-12in) apart. Cut lengths of looped blind tape to the same length as the blind. Stitch one length along each side seam, ensuring that the lowest loop is positioned 12cm (5in) from the bottom of the fabric. Stitch further tapes along the vertical divisions, keeping the loops parallel.

Making a casing
Turn up the bottom of the blind by 1cm (¹/4in) then a further 5cm (2in). Stitch the hem just below the lowest loops of the tapes to form a casing. Insert a length of narrow wooden lath and slip-stitch the ends.

Inserting the cords
Firmly tie a length of narrow nylon cord to the lowest loop on the first tape. Thread the cord up through the loops above, then run

it along the top and down the side of the blind. Thread cords through each of the tapes in the same way.

Fixing the blind to the batten
Fix screw eyes into the underside of the batten to line up with each of the tapes. Wrap the top of the blind over the batten and tack or staple it in place.

Starting from one side, thread each cord through the corresponding screw eye, then through each successive eye until all the cords are at one side edge. Knot the cords together and thread them through a cleat. When the cords are pulled, the blind will rise in a series of horizontal pleats.

POINTS TO CONSIDER

■ To ensure that the blind folds into sharp, neat pleats, you can stitch horizontal tucks across the width of the blind to correspond to alternate rows of loops on the tapes.

■ Ready-made blind tape has woven hoops which gives a standard-sized pleat. To achieve a wider or narrower effect, use plain tape and sew on small curtain rings.

■ The most suitable fabrics for this type of blind are lightweight cottons which drape easily. Thick fabrics are not suitable as they will not pleat effectively.

◀ *The horizontal pleats on a Roman blind are created by pulling up cords through vertical strips of looped blind tape. It is important to align the loops horizontally to ensure that the tension on each cord is equal, creating a sharp pleated finish (left).*

5
BATHROOMS

The bathroom may not be the most obvious place for fabric furnishings but, through the addition of just a few beautiful accessories, you can make a huge impact, transforming your bathroom into a place for relaxing as well as bathing.

Accessories can really set the mood of your bathroom. An eye-catching laundry bag will provide a practical and decorative place for dirty laundry, a hanging wall tidy with pockets is perfect for storing bottles and brushes in one place, and small wicker storage baskets can be given a pretty finishing touch with quilted liners.

Bathrooms are often small and so aim for a co-ordinated, streamlined look, keeping curtains and blinds simple and matching these to a shower curtain or under-sink valance.

5·1 SHOWER CURTAIN
5·2 LAUNDRY BAG
5·3 AUSTRIAN BLIND
5·4 HANGING WALL TIDY
5·5 FABRIC-LINED BASKET

5·1 SHOWER CURTAIN

It is not always possible to buy matching furnishings for your bathroom but, if you want your shower curtain to match blinds, curtains and other accessories, it is easy to make your own providing you waterproof the fabric thoroughly.

A matching valance is useful to disguise unsightly plumbing beneath the sink. This can be attached to the basin by a strip of self-adhesive touch-and-close fastener which allows it to be removed for cleaning.

Measuring and preparing the shower curtain
Measure the length of the curtain from just below the shower rail to half way down the bath or shower tray. Add 8cm (3¹/4in) for the top hem and 4cm (1¹/2in) for the bottom hem. For the width, measure the length of your curtain track and multiply this length 1¹/2-2 times depending on the required fullness of gathers. Treat the fabric with a waterproofing solution, following the manufacturer's instructions.

Sewing and hanging the curtain
Turn under and stitch a narrow 1.5cm (¹/4in) double hem down each side seam of the curtain. Turn a double 4cm (1¹/2in) hem to the wrong side of the fabric along the top edge and stitch it in place, close to the bottom fold. Turn and stitch a 1cm (¹/4in) and 3cm (1¹/2in) hem to the wrong side at the bottom of the curtain.

Mark positions for the clips at regular intervals along the top of the curtain and insert eyelets using an eyelet punch. Clip shower rings through the eyelets and thread the curtain onto the rail.

Measuring for an under-sink valance
For the width, measure the sides and the front of the basin and double this figure. For the drop, measure from just below the basin lip to the floor and add 8cm (3in) for the top heading and hem.

Hemming and hanging the valance
Turn under and slip-stitch narrow double hems along the sides and bottom of your

valance. Turn and press a 4cm (1¹/2in) hem to the wrong side along the top of the fabric. Cut a length of heading tape the same width as your valance, adding 2cm (³/4in) for turning under. Pin and stitch the heading tape just below the top edge of the valance, tucking under the raw edges of tape. Gather the heading to fit around the basin and attach a length of self-adhesive fastener over the heading tape. Stick the corresponding strip of fastener around the basin and press the valance into position.

POINTS TO CONSIDER

◼ As an alternative to waterproofing the shower curtain fabric, you can make a double layered curtain. This consists of an outer curtain in the fabric of your choice and an inner curtain of plain, waterproof material. Both curtains are measured and made up in the same way and the curtain rings are threaded through both sets of eyelets.

◼ Different looks for the valance can be achieved by using different curtain headings (see page 19). A pleated curtain gives a neat, streamlined alternative to the gathered basin valance.

◀ *An under-sink valance is a neat way to disguise unsightly plumbing. Simple to make, it is basically a standard curtain attached to the edge of the basin with touch-and-close fastening which enables it to be removed for easy cleaning (left).*

5·2 LAUNDRY BAG

Fabric bags are a simple storage solution for all manner of objects. In the bathroom, they are ideal as laundry or wash bags and they can be hand-decorated to suit any theme or decor.

These bags are quick and simple to make and can be made from fabric left over from larger projects. Most fabrics are suitable and it is possible to create a wide variety of looks ranging from small, delicate make-up bags to large, boldly-decorated toy bags for a child's room.

Cutting the fabric
Decide on the dimensions of your finished bag and cut out two rectangles of fabric adding a 1.5cm (1/2in) seam allowance on three sides and a 8cm (3in) allowance for the top casing. Draw and cut out paper templates for your chosen motifs and draw around these onto fabric. Cut out the shapes. Alternatively, you can cut out printed motifs from a large-patterned fabric.

Arrange the shapes on the right side of the fabric and tack them into position. Appliqué the shapes onto the bag fabric (see page 21).

Sewing the bag
Place the two rectangles of fabric together, right sides facing and seam around three sides, leaving the top open. Trim the seams and lower corners and oversew the raw edges of the hem to prevent the fabric from fraying (see page 17).

Making a casing
Press a 1cm (1/4in) single hem around the top of the bag to the wrong side of the fabric and then fold a 7cm (2 3/4in) hem. Form a casing by closing this hem with two rows of stitches; the first row being 3cm (1 1/4in) from the top and the second 3cm (1 1/4in) below.

Inserting the cord
Turn the bag the right way out and unpick the stitching between the two rows of

stitches along one seam. Cut a length of cord measuring just over twice the width of your bag. Attach a safety pin to one end of the cord and use this to ease the thread through the casing. Thread the cord through the channel to emerge at the same side seam opening.

Join the two ends of cord together, knotting them if the cord is narrow or binding them if it is thick. Ease the join into the casing and pull the cord to gather the top of the bag.

POINTS TO CONSIDER

■ These bags can be made in all sizes and can be given a unique feel depending on the fabric used. Tiny drawstring bags made from velvet can be filled with pot pourri and given as gifts or hung in wardrobes.

■ As an alternative to cord draw-string, make up narrow ties from fabric to match the bag. This can be easily done by cutting bias strips of fabric and stitching them to make a long tube.

▼ *A variety of looks can be created by using different fabrics and trimmings. Bold shapes appliquéd onto plain fabrics work well in the bathroom or a child's room. Velvet adds a touch of elegance, whereas patchwork and embroidery have a more rustic feel (below).*

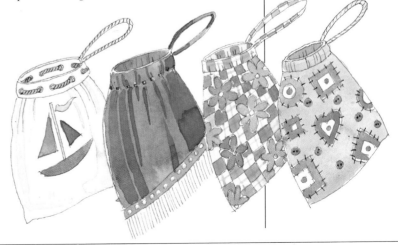

5·3 AUSTRIAN BLIND

Austrian blinds are pretty frilled blinds with soft gathers which add a feminine elegance to a window. The fabric is gathered at the top by a heading tape and then falls in loose swags created by vertical strips of corded tape.

A blind of this type needs to be fitted on a special Austrian blind track; this has a standard track to take the top heading and eyes on the underside to house the cords.

Measuring fabric
Measure the required drop of the blind from the track and add 4.5cm (2in) hem allowance. Measure the required width of the blind and multiply this measurement by 2-2^1/$_2$ to allow for gathers, adding an additional 3cm (1^1/4in) for the side seams. Cut the fabric to size, joining widths of material along the selvedges if necessary.

For the frill, measure around the bottom and two sides of your blind fabric and multiply this measurement by two. Cut a strip of fabric to this length and to the depth of the required frill, adding a 3cm (1^1/4in) seam allowance.

Attaching the frill
Stitch a narrow double hem along one long edge and two short sides of the frill piece. Along the remaining edge, sew a row of long machine stitch 1.5cm (1/2in) from the raw edge. Sew a second row of stitching 1cm (1/4in) below. Draw the threads so the frill fits around the blind. With right sides of fabric facing, pin and stitch the frill to the blind using a 1.5cm (1/2in) seam allowance. Trim and neaten the seam.

Applying tapes
Cut lengths of looped blind tape to the depth of your blind, ensuring that each piece has a loop positioned 1cm (1/4in) from one end. Position the strips at 25cm-30cm (10in-12in) intervals across the width of your blind, with the outside strips over the side seams. Pin and stitch the tapes onto the blind with the first loops 1cm (1/4in) from the bottom of the seam.

Fitting the blind
Turn over 3cm (1^1/4in) of fabric to the wrong side at the top of the blind and press. Stitch heading tape across the hem, covering the raw edge. Turn under the heading ends then gather the tape to fit the window.

Tie a length of cord to each bottom loop of the blind tape and thread it up through the loops above. Run the remaining end of the cord along the top of the blind and down the side. Fix the blind to an Austrian blind track and thread the loose ends of cord through a cleat. Pull the cords to create soft gathers in the blind.

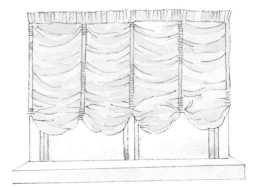

POINTS TO CONSIDER

■ Lightweight cottons and sheers are the most suitable fabrics for frilled blinds as they drape well and still allow sufficient light into a room.

■ Avoid lined or generously frilled blinds in a small, dark room as they will block out too much light and can look fussy.

■ A single line of looped tape and cord in the centre of a blind will pull up to create a fan-shaped tail of fabric either side. This creates an elegant and simple look for a large window and is suitable for use with sheer fabrics.

◄ *A festoon blind is made in a similar way to an Austrian blind. The vertical tapes are gathered tapes rather than corded tapes and these produce a ruched effect. A festoon blind has an added advantage in that it can be fitted onto a standard curtain track (left).*

5·4 HANGING WALL TIDY

A hanging storage tidy is a practical addition to any room and can be positioned on a wall, on the back of a door or in a cupboard. It can be made to suit the needs and style of any room, following the same basic method.

First decide on the dimensions of your wall tidy and its pockets; the one pictured here is 95cm (36in) long and 65cm (25in) wide, edged with a 2cm (3/4in) contrasting border. Each of the finished pockets measures 20cm (8in) wide and 22cm (8 1/2in) deep.

Measuring and cutting the fabric

Mark out the size of your tidy on a double thickness of fabric, adding a 1.5cm (1/2in) seam allowance to each side and cut it out.

For the side borders, cut two strips of fabric on the bias measuring 7cm (3in) deep and 3cm (1 1/4in) longer than the sides of the tidy. For the top and bottom casings, cut two strips of fabric measuring 8cm (3in) deep and 3cm (1 1/4in) wider than your tidy.

Sewing the main panel

Lay the two main pieces of fabric together, right sides out. With right sides together and raw edges matching, pin and stitch a strip of binding to each side edge of the fabric, using a 1.5cm (1/2in) seam allowance. Fold and press the binding over to the back, turn under the raw edges and slip-stitch it in place along the seam line.

Press 1.5cm (1/2in) of each short end of the casing strips over to the back of the fabric. Pin and sew the top and bottom casings to the main fabric in the same way as you applied the borders.

Making pockets

Mark the size of your pockets onto the main fabric, adding 9cm (3 1/2in) to the width and 3cm (1 1/4in) to the depth. Cut out the fabric and a piece of contrasting lining the same size for each one. With right sides facing, stitch the lining to the fabric leaving a gap for turning through. Press and trim the seams, turn each pocket the right way out and slip-stitch the opening.

To make side pleats, press back 3cm (1 1/4in) at the side of each pocket and top stitch from top to bottom right next to the fold. Align the edge of the pocket with the stitched fold to create a pleat and press firmly. Pin each pocket to the front of the tidy and stitch the sides of the pocket in place, directly below the fold. Stitch across the bottom of the pocket, sewing through all the thicknesses of fabric.

Insert a length of thin dowel in each casing and tie a length of decorative cord or rope to the top dowel as a hanger.

POINTS TO CONSIDER

■ PVC-coated fabric is a practical choice for a bathroom or child's room as it is waterproof and can be wiped clean easily.

■ Tailor the shape and size of pockets to suit their purpose. A child's tidy should have big pockets for toys and books, whereas a bedroom tidy can be made to carry shoes and accessories.

■ Pockets needn't be square or rectangular. A kitchen wall tidy could feature decorative vegetable pockets and, for a child's room, you could make a train-shaped wall hanging with pocketed carriages.

▼ *As an alternative to a cased heading, make a tab heading at the top of the tidy and suspend it from a decorative pole (below).*

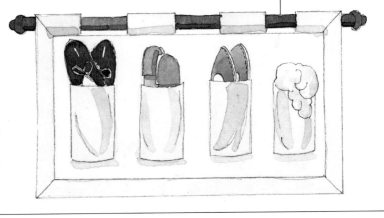

5·5 FABRIC-LINED BASKET

Wicker baskets of all shapes and sizes can be used to hold any amount of objects from toiletries to towels and linen. Both decorative and practical, they can be lined with fabric which co-ordinates with your decor.

For a neat finish, it is important that the fabric lining fits the basket perfectly and this is easily achieved using the base of the basket as a template. A fabric base is cut to this shape and then a section of gathered fabric is stitched around it to create the side of the lining. The completed liner can be decorated with braid, embroidery or quilting to make an ornate lining.

Cutting out fabric

Stand the basket on a piece of thin card and draw around it to make a template. Cut out two pieces of fabric to this shape, adding a 1.5cm (1/2in) seam allowance all around. Apply a layer of iron-on interfacing to one piece to give the base some body.

To make the pleated frill, measure the depth of the basket and multiply this measurement 1 1/2 times to create the overhang. Double the total depth measurement to cater for the double frill and add 3cm (1 1/4in) for seam allowances.

To calculate the width of the frill material, measure the circumference of the basket and double this measurement.

Making up the frill

With right sides of fabric facing, seam the short edges of the frill piece together to create a loop, using a 1.5cm (1/2in) seam allowance. Trim the seams and turn the fabric the right way out. Bring the two long raw edges together and press the fabric. Gather and press the raw edge into pleats to fit around the interlined base.

With right sides of fabric facing and raw edges even, pin the frill to the base piece, adjusting any pleats as necessary. Stitch the two together using a 1.5cm (1/2in) seam allowance. Trim the seam close to the stitching and oversew the raw edges (see page 16).

Stitching the base

Using tailor's chalk, draw a line following the curved shape of the base, 1cm (1/4in) in from the seam. Draw a further three lines 1cm (1/4in) apart and stitch over these lines using co-ordinating thread.

Fold and press under 1.5cm (1/2in) of fabric to the wrong side on the remaining base piece. Pin this to the back of the lined base and neatly slip-stitch it in place, enclosing the raw edges.

Fit the lining into the basket, folding the the top over the rim of the basket.

POINTS TO CONSIDER

▨ Take into account the size of the basket when choosing fabric. Plains or small prints work well on any size, whereas large, bold prints are best suited to larger baskets.

▨ Ensure the fabric you choose is washable as an open basket is sure to attract dust.

▼ *If lining a basket with a handle, make the frill in two sections so that it can be slotted around the handles.*

As an alternative to the pleated liner, the side fabric can be gathered onto the base. A casing at the top of the lining can be elasticated to give a snug fit over the rim of the basket. This fabric can then be extended and fitted with a second casing to house a draw-string cord (below).

6

BEDROOMS

Almost every surface in a bedroom can be accentuated with fabric, from the bed and headboard to windows and chairs. In addition, there are all types of accessories including screens, bolsters and canopies which can transform a plain bedroom into a restful haven.

The fabric you choose will depend on the atmosphere you wish to create. Draped laces and voiles add an air of romance, grand fabrics and draperies can create a more traditional, opulent look and a stark, contemporary feel can be conjured up with a wrought iron bed and clean cut linens.

Bedroom windows can be dressed in all manner of ways, ranging from frilled blinds teamed with floor length curtains or curtains with valances and tiebacks, to simple draped lengths of fabric. Whichever style you choose, you should ensure that it provides sufficient privacy and warmth in the room.

6.1 APPLIQUÉD DUVET COVER

The bed is usually the focal point of the bedroom and so your choice of bedding can dramatically alter the look of the room. Plain linen can be transformed by adding appliquéd motifs cut from remnants of fabric.

Fabric motifs can be applied to shop-bought bedding, but it is also simple to make your own duvet set.

Making a duvet cover
Measure your duvet and add a 1.5cm (1/2in) seam allowance to the top and sides and 8cm (31/4in) to the bottom. Cut two pieces of fabric to size. You may need to join fabric widths, in which case you should cut a central panel and join strips of fabric on either side, matching any patterning.

Turn under and sew a double 2.5cm (1in) hem at the bottom edge of each piece.

Adding appliqué
Cut out motifs from large-patterned fabric and pin them in position on the right side of the fabric. Appliqué around the edges of each shape (see page 21).

When you have completed the decoration, place the two pieces of fabric together with right sides facing and hemmed edges aligned. Stitch these together using a 2.5cm (1in) seam allowance for 30cm (12in) from either end, leaving a central opening. Remove the pins and tacking and sew press studs or buttons along the opening over the hemmed edges (see page 23). Turn the fabric the right way out and French seam the remaining three sides (see page 17).

Making a pillowcase
A standard pillowcase measures 75cm x 50cm (30in x 20in), but you can use the same method to make any size you wish. Cut a piece of fabric twice the length of your pillow, adding 26cm (101/4in) for turnings and 3cm (11/4in) to the width as seam allowance.

To create the front edge of the pillowcase, turn under 6.5cm (21/2in) along one short edge. Turn under the raw edge a further

6cm (21/4in) and stitch it into place through all thicknesses of fabric.

Turn under and sew a narrow double hem at the opposite end. Make a flap for the pillow at this end by folding 18cm (7in) of fabric over. Press the fold.

Apply the appliqué motifs as before, then fold the fabric in half widthways with wrong sides together and the wide-hemmed edge flush with the flap. Sew the sides of the pillowcase with French seams (see page 17).

POINTS TO CONSIDER

◼ The most practical fabric for making sheets, pillowcases and duvet covers is cotton or cotton mix material. This can be bought as sheeting which is available in an extra wide measure and saves having to join widths together, creating unsightly seams.

◼ Appliquéd motifs should be positioned carefully on pillowcases to prevent the stitching rubbing against the skin.

◼ Lace, ribbons and embroidery make pretty, decorative alternatives to appliqué.

◀ *As an alternative to surface decoration, you can add pretty piping and frilling into the seams when sewing your duvet set. Contrasting colours can be used for a contemporary look or self-coloured fabric for a more classic approach (left).*

6·2 BED CANOPY

In days gone by, curtains and canopies around a bed served a practical purpose in keeping out the cold. These days, they are purely decorative and can transform a plain divan into a wonderfully dramatic four-poster bed.

This basic wooden frame is made from lengths of timber and is attached to the divan for added stability. Because the curtains thread onto the top runners, these must be easily separated from the struts.

Measuring and cutting the curtains

Measure the length and width of the bed and double these measurements. Calculate the required drop of the canopy (see page 12) and add a 4.5cm (1¾in) hem allowance. Cut one piece of fabric for the head of the bed and two for the sides. Cut facings to the same width as each curtain piece and 10cm (4in) deep.

To calculate the tab length, measure the circumference of the runners and add an allowance for the tabs to be inserted into the heading. Decide on a tab width and double this measurement, adding two seam allowances. Cut as many tabs as you need.

Adding hems and headings

Stitch narrow double hems along the sides and bottoms of the curtains, mitring the corners neatly (see page 18). Sew narrow double hems along the sides of each facing.

Fold each tab in half lengthways with right sides together. Pin and stitch along one long side and trim the corners. Turn the fabric the right way out and press.

Constructing the curtains

Fold the tabs into loops and pin them along the right side of the curtain at regular intervals. Match the raw edges so the loops are inverted. Pin the facing on top, with the fabric right sides facing, sandwiching the tabs in between. Stitch along the top of the curtain through all the thicknesses of fabric, using a 1.5 (½in) seam allowance. Trim the seams, turn the fabric the right way out and press. Slip-stitch the bottom hem, then slip-

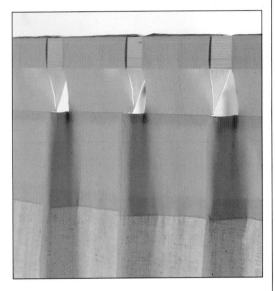

stitch the sides of the facing to the main fabric at either side of the curtain.

Hanging the canopy

Unscrew the frame one end at a time and slip the curtains onto the runners. The back curtain should hang down behind the bed and the side curtains can be left softly draped or secured with tiebacks.

POINTS TO CONSIDER

■ Calico is an ideal fabric for making a canopy as it is inexpensive and available in wide measures. It is a classic choice for all kinds of drapes.

■ Plain calico curtains can be decorated using stencils and fabric paint to co-ordinate with the room's decor.

■ If your fabric is light-coloured and needs regular cleaning, you might consider making tabs with buttons or press stud fastenings as a stitched tab-headed canopy can be difficult to launder as the bed frame will have to be dismantled each time to remove it.

◀ *As an alternative to using a wooden framework, the canopy fabric can be draped over two poles suspended from the ceiling. This type of canopy is made from one piece of fabric which has sewn in casings to house the poles (left).*

6·3 DRAPED MUSLIN CURTAINS

If privacy is not a priority, sheer curtains will provide a wonderfully light and airy feel to a window. The curtains can be classically simple or ornately decorative, and the softly draped fabric will reflect light into the room.

From the cheapest of muslins to the most beautiful of silks, draped fabrics make wonderful curtains. No special skills are needed to create a wonderfully sumptuous effect only patience, imagination and a long length of fabric.

Measuring fabric
Although there are no hard and fast rules concerning the amount of fabric required for a draped curtain, it is worth buying more than you think you will need, as any extra can be used to drape the curtains onto the floor in elegant folds. If you are using muslin, bear in mind that the fabric may not be pre-shrunk and you may need to allow extra for this. As a guide, approximately 5m (5¹/2yds) of fabric will give a good drape to an average size window.

The fabric should be ironed before use, although it is possible to spray the fabric with water once it is in place to 'damp out' any creases. Drape the fabric so that any pattern runs the right way up on the main drop. If necessary, join pieces of fabric along the selvedges to achieve the required width and length.

Finishing raw edges
Although sewing is not strictly necessary when making a draped curtain, it does help to oversew any raw edges to prevent the fabric from fraying, especially if it is going to be laundered. Fold and press narrow double hems along the raw edges and slip-stitch these in place.

Draping the curtain
Begin draping the curtain at one side of the window, leaving one end of the fabric so that it reaches down to the floor or drapes even further. Gently bunch the fabric and take it up over the front of the curtain pole,

loosely wrap it round twice, then drape it across the main window area.

To complete the look, wind the loose end of the fabric around the other end of the curtain pole and tie a wide, soft, decorative knot, enclosing any loose ends. When the curtain is in position, tease the fabric softly around the curtain pole to make several voluminous folds and drapes and to achieve the desired fullness.

POINTS TO CONSIDER

■ If you find that the fabric is prone to slipping whilst you are draping it, you can tack it in place at one end of a wooden curtain pole or use small pieces of touch-and-close fastener on a metal pole.

■ Muslin looks wonderful as a drape but can become limp and misshapen when washed. If you wash muslin, stretch it into shape and press it whilst damp.

■ For a practical window treatment, combine a blind with a drape of fabric in a co-ordinating colour.

▼ *A matching valance and curtains gives an airy feel to a window. The curtains can be tied onto the pole and the valance softly swathed in front to disguise any unsightly ends (below).*

6·4 BOLSTER CUSHIONS

Bolster cushions are a practical addition to a bedroom, adding firm support underneath or behind a pillow. They can also be used as a decorative feature and can be made in a wide variety of fabrics to suit your decor.

The long lines of bolster cushions make them particularly attractive as a finishing touch at the bedhead, especially when co-ordinated with a throwover bedspread. Quick and easy to make, bolsters can be fully fitted with flat ends, fitted with gathered ends or have a bag-like cover which is tied at each end like a cracker. You can choose from a wide variety of fabrics from opulent velvets to rich damasks or airy lightweight cottons. The simple draw-string bolsters pictured here are particularly suited to informal cotton fabrics which are easy to sew and naturally gather well.

Measuring your bolster cover
Measure the cushion pad to calculate the amount of fabric that you will require (see page 14). You will need to cut a rectangle of fabric as long and as wide as the pad, adding twice the diameter of the circular end to this length. You should also add a 1.5cm (1/2in) seam allowance to each side of the fabric.

Sewing the fabric
Cut out the cover and fold it right sides together, long edges matching. Pin the sides and stitch them together using a 1.5cm (1/2in) seam allowance. Press open the seam and finish the edges (see page 17). On the wrong side of the cover, fold a 1.5cm (1/2in) hem at both ends and stitch close to the edges to form casings. Leave an opening in the casings over the seam for threading through the cord.

Threading the cord
Cut a length of cord the same length as the diameter of your bolster cushion. Attach a safety pin to one end and use this to thread the cord through one casing. Pull the cord tight and knot the ends. Thread a second

length of cord through the casing at the opposite end. Insert the bolster pad into the cover and pull the ends of the cord to gather the end of the cover. Tie the cord in a neat bow and trim the ends.

Finishing touches
The ends of the cord can be left plain or finished with tassels, rosettes or beads as decoration. As an alternative to cord, you may wish to use pretty ribbons, ornate braiding or home-made piping.

POINTS TO CONSIDER

■ Choose fresh cotton fabrics for a contemporary look or silks and damasks in rich colours for a dramatic, luxurious effect.

■ A bag-like cover which ties over a bolster at both ends can add a romantic touch to a bedroom if made from white cotton lace fabric tied with pretty ribbon.

■ If you choose a heavy weave fabric, it is best to make a shaped bolster cover with a zip fastening and flat ends, as a heavy fabric will not draw up neatly into gathered ends.

▼ *Bolsters made with opulent fabrics such as velvets or damasks can add a touch of luxury to a bedroom. Trimmings such as piping, tassels and rosettes are particularly suited to this sumptuous look (below).*

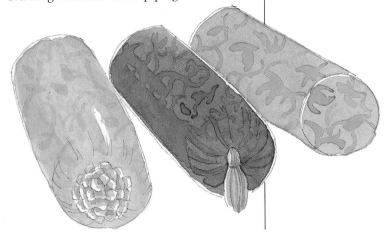

6.5 PATCHWORK QUILT

Patchwork is a time-honoured craft which has been passed down by generations of women. Traditionally it was an activity which brought the community together, both as a social event and as a practical way of producing home furnishings.

Patchwork is a time-consuming activity but the beautiful results are well worth the effort expended and a quilt can be passed down as an heirloom to your family.

Making templates
For classic hexagonal patchwork, you will need to draw and cut out two hexagonal templates, one measuring 8cm (3¹/4in) across for the fabric, and the other 6cm (2³/4in) for paper liners. Cut out as many fabric and paper hexagons as you need.

Inserting the liners
Lay a paper liner in the centre of the wrong side of each fabric hexagon. Fold over the seam allowance and tack it to the paper.

Joining the patches
Place two patches together, right sides facing, aligned along one edge. Oversew the matched edges with small, neat stitches. Build up the pattern by joining more patches in the same way.

Make 'flowers' by joining six patches of the same colour fabric in a ring. Add a different coloured patch to the centre and in between the flowers, and use half hexagons to fill gaps and make straight edges. Once completed, press the patchwork and remove the tacking and paper liners.

Constructing the quilt
Cut a piece of backing fabric and wadding to the same size as the patchwork panel. Lay the wadding on the wrong side of the backing and place the patchwork right side up on top. Pin the layers together and, starting at the centre, tack a line of stitches along the width and length of the quilt. Tack across the diagonals and around the edges, then remove the pins and trim away any excess backing and wadding.

Adding the border and quilting
For the border, cut strips of fabric twice the required depth plus 1.5cm (¹/2in) seam allowances, and longer than each of the sides of your quilt. Mitre the corners of the border fabric (see page 18). With right sides facing, stitch one edge of the border to the quilt. Fold the border to the back of the quilt, turn under the raw edges and slip-stitch it in place along the seam line.

To finish the quilt, stitch around each flower and the border approximately 6mm (¹/4in) from the edge. Remove the tacking.

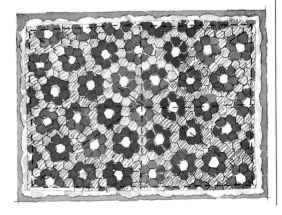

POINTS TO CONSIDER

▓ Although patchwork can be made from a variety of fabrics, it is best to start with cottons which are lightweight, firmly woven and easy to sew. Wash the fabric beforehand to ensure that it is pre-shrunk and vary the different types of fabric all over the quilt to ensure a balanced result.

▓ Patchwork can be made with shapes of any size, varying from regular shapes of the same size to individual pieces which are cut to fit the surrounding shapes. For your first quilt, it is best to stick to squares or hexagons which easily fit together.

▓ Patchwork is absorbing and relaxing to make, but it is not for the impatient. If you are unsure whether you have the patience to make a quilt, you could try a smaller project such as a cushion cover first.

◀ *When attaching a backing to a project of this size, it can be difficult to achieve a flat, neat finish. Starting from the centre, you should tack a vertical and horizontal line of stitches, then sew across the diagonals and around the outside edge. This will hold all the thicknesses of fabric firmly in place (left).*

6·6 BLANKET BOX

Blanket boxes can be used to store all kinds of linens and can double as a flat display area. As well as creating a useful storage space, they can add a decorative touch to a room if they are attractively covered.

An inexpensive melamine storage box can be transformed into an attractive blanket box with fabric and trimmings. It may be unlined or you can add a layer of covered wadding to make a sumptuous interior.

Covering the box
If possible, remove the lid from the top of the blanket box. Cut a piece of fabric to fit around the box, allowing extra for turning under. Starting from the back, wind the fabric around the box. Fold a narrow hem and staple the fabric in position, marking the hinge screw holes with pins.

Turn the box on its side. Fold the fabric under the box with a narrow double hem and staple it neatly around the bottom. Cover the top edge in the same way, ensuring that the fabric is folded neatly around the box rim. Glue a length of decorative braid over the stapled edge.

Covering the lid
Cut a piece of fabric to cover the lid, adding extra for turning under. Cut a piece of wadding to fit the top of the lid. Position the wadding and lay the fabric over it. Staple the fabric to the underside of the lid, approximately 5cm (2in) from the edge, pulling the fabric taut. Trim away any excess fabric.

Cut a piece of lining for the underside of the lid and trim 1.5cm (1/2in) from around the edges. Fold under a narrow hem and staple the lining to the bottom of the lid. Cover the edge with braid. Replace the hinges and fix the lid to the box.

Making a pelmet
To make the pelmet, cut a length of self-adhesive card to fit around the box. Shape the bottom edge of the card at the desired depth. Lay the card onto a piece of fabric

and cut around it, adding a 1.5cm (1/2in) seam allowance. Place the fabric on a flat surface, wrong side up and remove the backing from the card. Smooth the card sticky side down onto the fabric.

Remove the backing from the reverse of the card and fold the raw edges of the fabric over, snipping the edges to fit around the curves. Fix the pelmet to the box using touch-and-close fastener. Stitch a tassel to the lid as a finishing touch.

POINTS TO CONSIDER

▦ Make a removable, washable lining for a blanket box by sewing a fitted lining and attaching it around the inside rim of the box with touch-and-close fastener.

▦ You can trim a blanket box with all kinds of decorative finishes. Add buttons to the lid for a classic look or deep fringing to the base for a traditional feel.

▦ Most fabrics are suitable for this type of project. Light-coloured cottons give an airy feel, whereas rich velour or tapestry has a sumptuous classic effect.

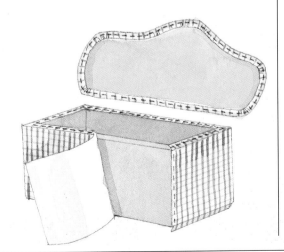

◀ *A fabric covering is simple to apply to an inexpensive plain blanket box. The main box is covered with just one piece of fabric which is wrapped around and stapled in place. The lid is softly padded and covered with a contrasting fabric. The raw edges are covered with lining fabric and braid for a neat finish (left).*

6·7 PADDED HEADBOARD

A padded headboard will add a touch of comfort to your bedroom and make a useful backrest. This headboard is filled with lightweight wadding and suspended by fabric ties from a co-ordinating curtain pole above the bed.

Each panel of the headboard is a similar size to a standard pillow and so you should cut a paper template measuring 75cm x 50cm (30in x 20in). Round the corners of the template, then cut four pieces of fabric adding 1.5cm (1/2in) seam allowances all around. To make a frill for each, cut a fabric strip measuring twice as long as the perimeter of one of your main pieces and 17cm (6³/4in) wide.

Sewing the frill
With right sides together, pin and stitch the short ends of each strip of fabric to form a loop. Press the loop in half lengthways with wrong sides together. Sew a line of gathering stitches through both layers of fabric along the long raw edge. Pull up the thread to fit the frill around the headboard, leaving extra fabric in the corners so the frill lies flat.

Attaching the frill
Make up enough covered piping for each headboard piece (see page 18). With right sides facing and raw edges matching, pin and tack the piping, then the frill around one of the main fabric pieces. Butt the ends of the piping together and attach the frill using a zipper foot.

Making ties
Cut four strips of fabric measuring 40cm x 10cm (16in x 4in). Fold the strips in half lengthways with right sides together and stitch along the long seam and across the top raw edges using a 1.5cm (1/2in) seam allowance. Trim the seams, turn the ties through and press.

Constructing the headboard
Cut a piece of wadding for each headboard. Pin one piece to the wrong side of each of

the remaining main fabric pieces. With right sides facing and raw edges matching, tack the headboard pieces together, enclosing the frill and piping. Tack each pair of ties into place 10cm (4in) from the corners and sew through all the layers with a zipper foot, using a 1.5cm (1/2in) seam allowance. Leave an opening at the bottom for turning through. Trim the seams, turn the fabric through and slip-stitch the openings.

POINTS TO CONSIDER

▨ Take care when positioning the pole that it is high enough not to cause any discomfort when resting against the headboard. The pole should be trimmed so that its length is in proportion to your bed.

▨ A looped heading can be stitched to the back of each pillow as an alternative to ties. The pillows will then simply slot onto the pole.

▨ For a more streamlined look, make one large headboard which drapes over a pole and is tied together at the sides with narrow bindings.

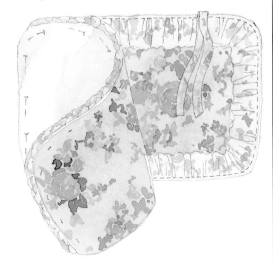

◄ *The soft wadding for the headboard is pinned to the wrong side of one of the main fabric pieces. The frill, piping and ties are tacked onto the right side of the second main piece and all the components are sewn in place at the same time (left).*

6·8 FABRIC-COVERED SCREEN

A beautiful screen can serve as both a decorative and practical feature in a bedroom. The panels can be covered in rich, dense fabric for an opulent look or a delicate framework can be stretched with translucent fabric giving a light, airy feel.

A screen is generally made of a number of wooden panels which are hinged together. The panels come in a variety of styles; they may simply be rectangular or shaped with soft curves or arches and can be solid wood or MDF (medium density fibreboard). Some have a lighter framework with one or two crossbars for support. The screen panels are not difficult to cover, but it is well worth investing in a staple gun to make the job as straightforward and simple as possible.

Measuring a screen
It is possible to obtain blank screen panels which are ready to cover from specialist craft and hobby suppliers or, if you draw up a template, your local timber merchant should be able to cut panels to size for you. There are no hard and fast rules concerning the size of the panels, although the screen should stand tall enough to provide practical use as a divide for a dressing area or to add interest to a bare corner. A standard height of 1.5m (5ft) is a good starting point with a corresponding panel width of 50cm (20in).

Cutting out fabric
Using one screen panel as a template, lay the fabric on a flat surface and place the screen on top. Draw round it using tailor's chalk, adding an extra 1cm (1/2in) all round for turning over. Cut out two fabric pieces for each panel, keeping any patterns central.

Covering the panels
Lay one fabric piece onto a screen panel, ensuring that the straight grain of the fabric runs in line with the vertical of the panel. Staple the fabric to the narrow edge of the screen panel, making sure that the fabric is straight and taut across the panel. Trim the fabric if necessary so that the raw edge is even around the edge of the frame. Turn the panel over and attach fabric to the reverse of the screen in the same way. Cover the remaining panels in the same way.

Trimming the edges
Once the panels are covered on both sides, the raw edges around the screen can be trimmed with gimp or braid. Choose braid which is the same width as the edge of your panels. To avoid making ugly joins, calculate the amount of braid you will need before you begin.

Begin at the bottom edge of each panel and work your way around the border, gluing the braid firmly in place as you go, using a strong fabric adhesive. Allow the glue to dry thoroughly.

Assembling your screen
When the glue is dry, replace the hinges on one panel, screwing them firmly in place. Stand the second panel next to it and mark the position of the hinges, ensuring that the screen will stand square. Join the two, then add subsequent panels in the same way.

▼ *Basic screen panels are easy to cover with fabric. The raw edges of the fabric are secured along the panel border and then disguised by a length of contrasting braid or gimp (below).*

7.
CHILDREN'S ROOMS

When furnishing a children's room you can be as lively and imaginative as you like, using fabrics which are bursting with colour and pattern. However, it is important to remember that furnishings for young children and toddlers must be made with safety in mind, avoiding ties, buttons or any trimmings which could be easily swallowed or cause danger.

Ornate fairy tale curtains and bed canopies look wonderful but, if the room is to double as a playroom, all the fabrics will need to be hard-wearing and washable. It is the little accessories that can make the room really special. Co-ordinating liners for toy baskets, decorative shelf liners, wall hangings and picture frames all add up to a lively overall effect. More ambitious projects, such as duvet covers and patchwork quilts can be scaled down to suit a child's size, with the added advantage of being quick and simple to make.

7·1 PRINCESS BED CANOPY

Little girls will love this beautiful canopy which transforms a plain divan into a bed fit for a princess. Choose bold nursery prints for a contemporary look or the sheerest of muslins or voiles for a light, fairy tale effect.

The curtains and pelmet of this canopy hang from a small shelf measuring 46cm x 15cm x 2cm (18in x 6in x 3/4in). This shelf is fitted to the wall above the bed at a height of 180cm (72in) and is supported by metal brackets. You will need to fix six screw eyes to the underside of the shelf; one in each corner and two at the centre front.

Measuring fabric for the curtains
For the drop of each side curtain, measure from the shelf to the floor and add 16cm (6½in). For the width, measure along one short side and halfway along one long side of the shelf. Double this measurement and add a 3cm (1¼in) seam allowance. The lining should measure the same length as the main curtain, but be 10cm (4in) wider.

For the backdrop, cut a piece of lining fabric as long as the drop from the shelf to the floor plus 7cm (3in). The fabric should be 1½ times the width of the bed.

Lining the curtains
With right sides facing and raw edges matching, pin the lining to the curtains. Sew the long edges using a 1.5cm (½in) seam allowance, then trim and press the seams. Turn the fabric the right way out and press the extra lining to form a border down the front edge of each curtain.

Sew a narrow double hem at the bottom of each curtain then turn under 5cm (2in) at the top. Stitch heading tape over the raw edges at the top of each curtain, tucking under the raw ends of tape. Gather the tape and tie the strings at either end.

Hemming the backdrop
Sew 1.5cm (½in) hems along the sides and bottom edge of the backdrop. Turn under 1cm (¼in) then a further 3cm (1¼in) at the top, stitching the edges to form a casing.

Hanging the curtains
Thread the backdrop onto curtain wire and attach this to the screw eyes at the back of the shelf. Pull up the tapes to fit the curtains around the shelf. Add curtain hooks and fix the curtains to the remaining screw eyes.

Making a pelmet
Cut a piece of self-adhesive card to fit around the shelf, shaping the bottom edge. Cover the card with fabric, folding under the raw edges. Fold the sides of the pelmet to fit around the shelf and fix it in place using touch-and-close fastener.

POINTS TO CONSIDER

■ If your pelmet is heavy, it can be reinforced with small tacks at each side to give added support.

■ You can adjust the length of the curtains to create different effects. You will need more material if you intend the curtains to drape elegantly on the floor or if you intend to use tiebacks.

■ A princess canopy might not be the first choice for a boy, but this design can be adapted to make a fun tipi.

◀ *The curtains of this pretty canopy have a gathered heading which is hooked onto six screw eyes fixed to the underside of a small shelf. A pelmet, cut from self-adhesive card and covered with contrasting fabric, disguises the shelf and gives a neat, professional finish (left).*

7·2 PLAY TENT

This tipi-style tent has an inexpensive calico cover which is threaded with bean poles to create the frame. The tent is suitable for use in and out of doors and can be decorated using bright, colourful fabric paints.

The tent cover is made from five triangular panels for which you will need to make a pattern. On a sheet of paper, draw an isosceles triangle measuring 95cm (38in) wide at the base and 145cm (58in) tall. Cut 6cm (2½in) from the top of the triangle and gently curve the base line. Use the pattern to cut four panels of fabric, adding a 1.5cm (½in) seam allowance all around. Cut a fifth panel in the same way, adding an extra 3cm (1¼in) to one long side.

Making loops
To make the fabric loops which carry the drawstring, cut a bias strip of fabric measuring 50cm x 5cm (20in x 2in). Press it in half with right sides facing to form a long strip. Stitch along the long raw side using a 1.5cm (½in) seam allowance. Press and trim the seam, then turn the fabric the right way out. Cut the strip into six equal pieces.

Making a facing
Using the top of the panel pattern, cut a narrow facing for each panel, measuring the same width and 3cm (1¼in) deep. Fold a narrow bottom hem to the wrong side of each piece. With right sides together, stitch the top of each facing to the top of a panel, sandwiching the end of one loop piece in between. Turn the fabric the right way and slip-stitch the bottom of the facing on the wrong side of the panel. Bring the free end of the loop over to the right side, tuck under the raw edge and sew it in place.

Joining the panels
Turn and sew a narrow double seam along one long edge of one panel to make the door. With right sides of fabric uppermost, lay two same-size panels side by side, overlapping the edges by 6cm (2½in). Fold under the raw edge of the overlap, using a

1.5 (½in) seam allowance and stitch the two panels together close to the fold. Turn over the fabric pieces and hem the raw edge of the overlap on the back in the same way to form a casing. Join the remaining panels in the same way, positioning the door panel at one end with its seamed edge outermost and the wider panel on the opposite side. Turn 3cm (1¼in) of the wider panel to the wrong side of the fabric and stitch it in place to form an outside casing.

Adding the drawstring
Cut a strip of fabric measuring 1m x 5cm (40in x 1½in). Turn and press a narrow hem along the long sides. Fold the strip in half lengthways with right sides facing and stitch across both short ends. Press the seams and turn the strip the right way out. Press it lengthways and stitch the long sides together, using a 3mm (⅛in) seam allowance. Thread the drawstring through the loops.

Insert a bean pole into each casing. Pull up and tie the ends of the drawstring to hold the poles together.

POINTS TO CONSIDER

▦ Using the same basic design, cut windows into two of the panels and decorate the fabric with painted shutters and window boxes for a pretty Wendy house style tent.

▦ For safety reasons, ensure that children are supervised at all times when using bean poles or canes.

▼ *This tipi-style tent is made from five triangular panels of calico. The panel pieces are overlapped to create casings which house the bean pole framework (below).*

7·3 SHELF LINERS

The addition of decorative shelf borders adds a fun finishing touch to plain shelves in a child's room. The liners can be cut into any shape and are an ideal way of using up remnants of fabric.

Shelf liners can be made to suit almost any room in the house, using fabric which complements the environment. Chintzy cottons can be used on a kitchen dresser to create a country cottage feel, delicate laces or crochets add a romantic touch to a bedroom, whilst bright, contemporary prints can be used to make fun liners for a children's room.

Measuring the fabric

Measure around the sides and front of the shelf to calculate the amount of fabric required. The depth of a liner is a purely personal choice, but it should be kept in proportion to the shelf. You also need to consider the fabric pattern and ensure that it fits comfortably within the chosen depth. For example, plain or all-over patterns such as dots and stripes can be cut to any depth but, if the fabric has a definite repeat pattern, this should be used as a guide to the depth of the liner.

Covering the liner

Draw the outline of the liner onto self-adhesive card, adding a decorative border along the bottom edge. Cut out the shape and remove the backing paper from one side. Lay the fabric flat and smooth the card onto the fabric sticky side down, keeping any patterning central.

Cut away the excess fabric from around the liner, leaving a narrow 1.5cm (1/2in) border for turning over. Remove the remaining backing paper and fold over the raw edges of the fabric, clipping into any curves to allow the fabric to lie flat.

Adding lining

Using the shelf liner as a template, draw and cut out the shape from contrasting fabric to make the lining. Fold under a narrow seam

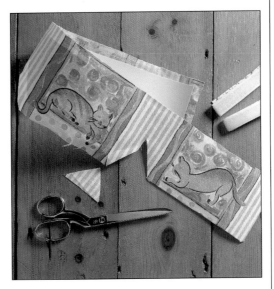

allowance around the lining and press it into place. Position the lining on the back of the shelf liner and glue or slip-stitch it neatly into place.

Attaching the liner to the shelf

Gently curve the liner around the edges of the shelf. Mark the position of the sides of the shelf at the top of the liner and then fold over the sides to fit around the shelf.

Apply one side of a length of touch-and-close fastener along the top edge on the back of the liner. Attach the corresponding side of the fastener to the rim of the shelf and press the liner into position.

POINTS TO CONSIDER

■ Choose fabric which suits the theme of a room and add suitable trimmings. A length of rope glued around the shelf rim can add a jaunty, nautical look to a bathroom.

■ The bottom edge of a liner can be cut into to create a wide range of effects. Use a template to draw the pattern to ensure a neat, even finish.

▼ *A shelf liner is a simple way to disguise an ugly shelf. A simple pelmet of fabric is attached to the shelf rim using a strip of touch-and-close fastening (below).*

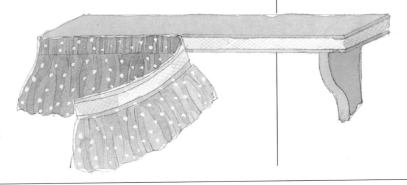

7·4 CIRCUS TENT WARDROBE

This fun wardrobe makes a lively addition to any child's room. Its framework is a standard shelving unit and you can adapt any self-assembly book shelf or even construct your own. The fabric covering can be easily removed for cleaning.

To make the roof, cut two pieces of MDF (Medium Density Fibreboard) to the same width as the unit and two thirds the length of the top shelf. Mitre the edges, then place the boards on top of the unit to form the roof. Nail the boards together at the point where they meet and to the sides of the shelf unit. Fix a hanging rail below the top shelf.

Measuring the fabric
For the main cover, cut a piece of fabric measuring the same depth as the unit and wide enough to fit around the sides and back from the left to the right-hand upright. Add a 2cm (3/4in) seam allowance to each side of the fabric.

For the front curtain, cut a piece of contrasting fabric to the same dimensions as the shelf unit opening, adding a seam allowance. To cover the roof, cut a piece of fabric the same width and twice as long as one of the roof pieces. Cut a fabric triangle to cover the back space. For the front flaps, cut two triangles equal to the size of the back triangle, adding a 1.5cm (1/2in) seam allowance all round.

Covering the unit
Press under the seam allowance on the main cover and sew one side of a length of touch-and-close fastener around all the edges. Attach the other strip around the top and bottom of the shelf unit and along the front uprights. Fix the cover in position.

Sew narrow double hems around the curtain and sew a strip of touch-and-close fastener along the top of the curtain. Stick the corresponding side of the fastener above the opening and fix the curtain in place.

Covering the roof
With right sides facing and raw edges matching, sew the back triangle to the long

roof piece. Turn under and press the raw edges. Join the front flaps to the roof piece using a 2cm (3/4in) seam allowance. Press and hem all the raw edges.

Adding the trim
Cut a strip of fabric wide enough to fit around the base of the roof section. With right sides facing, seam the trim. Cut zigzags into the edge of the trim using pinking shears. Slip the cover over the roof section to complete the wardrobe.

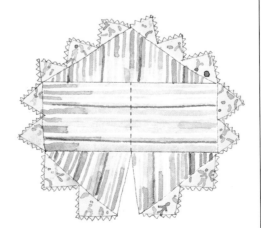

POINTS TO CONSIDER

■ If you are making the wardrobe for a small child's room, it is best to fix it to the wall so it cannot topple over.

■ Instead of removing the shelves to create hanging space, the unit can be left intact and used as a toy cupboard.

■ Lightweight, washable fabrics are most suitable for a child's room. Choose fabrics which co-ordinate with the decor or bold, deckchair stripes for a seaside effect.

◀ *The roof section for this fun wardrobe is made from a strip of fabric which runs the length of the roof piece. An enclosed triangular section fits across the back of the roof piece and two triangular pieces are fitted to the front which can be drawn back to allow access to the upper storage area (left).*

7·5 NOVELTY PILLOW

Making cushions for a child's room gives you the opportunity to be really creative. You can make cushions in any shape, using the boldest, brightest fabrics available. Small cushions can be made for toys and larger cushions make perfect bean bags.

This flower cushion adds a dash of colour to a child's bedroom. For the best results, make a paper template to ensure that all the pieces fit together before you begin.

Making a template

Draw around a large dinner plate to make a template for the centre of the flower. To make a template for the petals, fold a piece of paper in half and cut a gentle curve in one side. The petals may be short and wide or long and thin, so long as they fit closely together around the flower centre. When you have cut your petal template, use the plate to draw a gentle curve in one end.

Cutting fabric

Pin the templates to the fabric. Cut two flower centres and two pieces of fabric for each petal, adding a 1.5cm (¹/₂in) seam allowance all around. Cut corresponding shapes from wadding; for a plumper cushion, the flower centre can be filled with a piece of foam rubber. A contrasting coloured piping adds a bolder finish to the edge of the cushion. Make up enough cord piping to edge each petal (see page 20).

Inserting piping

Starting at the bottom edge of each petal, with right sides facing and raw edges matching, pin a length of piping around the shape. Lay the second petal shape on top, right sides facing, sandwiching the piping between the two layers of fabric. Lay the wadding on top and tack the layers together using a 1.5cm (¹/₂in) seam allowance.

Using a zipper foot, stitch through the tacking line, leaving the bottom of each petal open for turning through. Trim the seams, clipping the seam allowance around the curves and press the seams open. Turn the petals the right way out.

Sewing the cushion

Lay a flower centre right side up on the circular wadding. Pin the petals in position with the raw edges matching so the petals point inward. Lay the remaining fabric piece on top, right sides facing and stitch around the outside through all layers of fabric at the same time using a 1.5cm (¹/₂in) seam allowance. Leave an opening for turning through.

Trim the seams, clipping the curves and press them open. Turn the cushion the right way out and slip-stitch the opening closed.

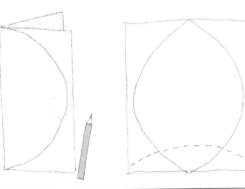

◀ *You can ensure a symmetrical shape for the petals by cutting the template from a folded piece of paper. The petals can be any width or length so long as they fit closely together around the flower centre (left).*

FABRIC GLOSSARY

Although you will find that the person selling you a fabric will be able to advise you on its use, some prior knowledge of fabric types will enable you to make an informed choice. A selection of the most commonly-found fabrics are listed here.

Brocade
This is a crisp, satin weave fabric which has a raised floral design. This is created by the warp or weft threads which are floated over the surface giving an ornate, embroidered look. Brocade can be used for curtains, cushions and some upholstery projects.

Broderie Anglaise
This is a light woven cotton with pretty embroidered holes and patterns. It can be used for decorative bed linens or bedroom cushions and bolsters.

Buckram
This stiff, lightweight, coarse woven cotton cloth is most commonly used as a stiffening agent for linings and pelmets.

Bump
This is a wadding material made from raised cotton waste and used between lining and fabric to give body, weight and warmth to curtains. It is also known as 'interlining'.

Calico
An inexpensive, woven cotton fabric which is lighter than canvas. Most commonly, it is available in a natural cream colour, but it can also be bleached white or dyed in a wide range of colours.

Canvas
This strong, durable fabric is sometimes woven from linen and occasionally from synthetic fibres. It comes in a variety of weights and it may also be referred to as 'cotton duck'.

Chenille
This is a luxurious pile fabric made from a special fancy yarn which has tufts projecting out from all around the central thread. It has a soft, luxurious feel suitable for making chair throws and bed spreads.

Chintz
This close weave cotton fabric can be either printed or plain. It often has a glazed finish which gives it a characteristic sheen which repels dust and dirt.

Crushed velvet
The pile of this velvet cloth is treated during finishing to flatten it in different directions. This creates permanent, irregular creases which form a decorative feature.

Damask
This self-coloured, satin-finished fabric has traditional floral designs woven into the surface. It is available in a variety of natural and synthetic fibres.

Denim
Although most commonly associated with jeans and overalls, this tough, cotton twill weave cloth has become fashionable for creating inexpensive, hard-wearing cushions and upholstery.

Flannelette
Similar to wincyette but heavier, flannelette is a cotton version of the wool cloth, flannel. Flannelette has a soft nap on both sides which makes it ideal for making winter bedding.

Gingham

This traditionally woven, checked fabric has a checked pattern formed by dyed yarns spaced regularly in both the warp and weft threads. The most common colour way is a combination of white and a contrasting colour. It is usually made from cotton or mixed cotton and synthetic fibres.

Lace

Originally made by hand from linen, modern lace is usually machine-manufactured using nylon, viscose or cotton threads. It is most commonly either white or cream in colour and its delicate patterning makes it an ideal choice for tablecloths and café curtains.

Linen

This strong cloth is woven from flax fibres and is prone to shrinkage and creasing if not mixed with another fibre. Linen union is a mix of linen and cotton and is usually strengthened with a percentage of nylon. Linen is available either plain or printed.

Muslin

This is a very soft, semi-transparent fabric with a gauzy texture which is often used for draped window treatments.

Net

A transparent curtain fabric made from cotton or synthetic yarns knotted together to form a mesh. It does not fray when cut.

Raw silk

A natural fibre sometimes known as wild silk which is spun then woven into soft fabric with a slubby, coarse texture.

Sateen

A soft cotton fabric with a slight surface sheen. It is available in different weights ranging from fine lining sateen to heavy curtaining fabric.

Silk

A strong, natural luxury fibre woven from the filament surrounding cocoons made by silk worms. Wild silk is characteristically irregular whilst cultivated silk produces a smooth, even textured fabric.

Tapestry

This is a heavy, woven fabric often showing a traditional pictorial design. It is suitable for cushions, screens, wall hangings and upholstery.

Tartan

A traditionally woven fabric in two or more colours creating a checked cloth. Originating from Scotland, individual designs are associated with specific Scottish families or clans.

Ticking

This robust cotton twill fabric is traditionally used for pillows, bolsters and mattress covers.

Toile de jouy

This traditional cotton fabric features a printed design in one colour against a natural or off-white background. By tradition, the designs often depict rustic scenes or figures.

Velvet

A soft, luxurious warp pile fabric with a dense, short pile. Made from cotton or man-made fibres, it is difficult to handle.

Velveteen

Similar to velvet although easier to sew, velveteen is usually made from cotton with a pile running across the weave.

Voile

A fine, lightweight fabric made from cotton or synthetic yarns. Plain or patterned, it is ideal for sheer curtains as it drapes well.

FABRIC CARE

Home furnishings are subjected to daily wear and tear and may soon look shabby if not cared for properly. Washable fabrics should be laundered regularly and you should take on-the-spot action to remove potential stains as and when they occur.

To prevent permanent marking, stains and spillages should be acted upon quickly, using a tried and tested remedy or appropriate stain remover. If the fabric is delicate or if you are in any doubt about how to remove a stain, seek advice from a dry cleaner or fabric retailer.

Here are some of the most common stain problems and some simple solutions:

Alcohol
Washable fabrics: Rinse fresh stains in warm water then wash using a biological detergent. On red wine, pour on a small amount of white wine, then soak before washing. Treat dried stains on whites with a mild bleach solution or with a white vinegar solution on coloureds. Soak and wash using a biological detergent.
Non-washable fabrics: Blot then sponge the stain with lukewarm water. Spirit marks can be removed using washing up liquid which is then wiped off with warm water. Blot the fabric dry. Fresh wine marks should be sponged then sprinkled with talcum powder. Brush the powder off after a few minutes.

Blood
Washable fabrics: Soak the stain as soon as possible in cold, salty water or biological detergent, then wash in cool water. Soak stubborn stains in a hydrogen peroxide solution, adding a few drops of ammonia.
Non-washable fabrics: Sponge with cold water and rinse, adding a few drops of ammonia. Use a proprietary cleaner to remove persistent marks or have the item professionally dry cleaned.

Candle wax
Washable fabrics: Scrape off the excess, then place blotting paper both under and over the stain. Press with a warm iron, allowing the paper to absorb the wax. Repeat with new paper until most of the wax is displaced. Wash the item using a biological detergent.
Non-washable fabrics: Remove the wax with paper and a warm iron then wipe the area with warm water and blot dry.

Chewing gum
Washable and non-washable fabrics: Harden the gum by applying ice cubes or, if the item is small, put it in the fridge. Once hard, the gum should be easy to crack and pull off. Remove the last remnants with a dry cleaning liquid. Clean washable fabrics in the normal way.

Chocolate
Washable fabrics: Blot or scrape off the excess and wash the item with a warm biological detergent.
Non-washable fabrics: Blot off the excess, then sponge with warm detergent or a mild borax solution. When dry, treat the stain with a spot remover or have the item dry cleaned professionally.

Grass
Washable fabrics: Apply methylated spirits before rinsing with warm water. Soak and wash in a biological detergent solution.
Non-washable fabrics: Dab with methylated spirits and sponge with a mild detergent solution. Blot dry and dry clean if necessary.

Grease, fat and oil
Washable fabrics: Scrape off the excess and dab with washing up liquid. Wash in a warm detergent solution. On delicate fabrics, dab the stain with eucalyptus oil then wash. Bad stains should be soaked in a soda solution before washing. Remove any remaining traces with a spot remover.
Non-washable fabrics: Apply a dry cleaning solution at home or have bad stains dry cleaned professionally.

Lipstick and mascara
Washable and non-washable fabrics: Dab the stain with methylated spirits then a little washing up liquid. Rinse with warm water.

Mildew and mould
Washable fabrics: Wash the item several times using a biological detergent. Whites and cottons can be treated with a mild bleach solution.
Non-washable fabrics: Sponge the area with a mild detergent solution and rinse. Dry clean if necessary.

Milk
Washable fabrics: Rinse well in lukewarm water, then wash using a biological detergent. Soak dried stains before washing.
Non-washable fabrics: Sponge with lukewarm water and treat with a proprietary grease solvent when dry.

Nail varnish
Washable fabrics: Blot off any excess, then dab with nail varnish remover. Use methylated spirits to remove any remaining colour. On acetate fabrics, you should use amyl acetate.
Non-washable fabrics: Take the item to a dry cleaners for professional stain removal.

Paint
Washable fabrics: Scrape off any excess immediately. If the paint is water-based, sponge or rinse the stain with cold water then wash as normal. Use methylated spirits on dried stains or to remove remaining traces of colour. If the paint is oil-based, apply white spirit, then sponge and wash using a biological detergent.
Non-washable fabrics: Sponge water-based paint with cold water and blot dry. Oil-based paints should be dabbed with white spirit. If the stain is persistent, seek professional advice.

Scorch marks
Washable fabrics: Rinse in cold water and soak in a warm borax solution before washing. Stubborn marks may respond to bleaching with a hydrogen peroxide solution, but test the fabric beforehand to ensure that it can withstand such treatment. Bad scorch marks are irreparable.
Non-washable fabrics: Seek professional advice from a fabric manufacturer or professional dry cleaner.

Urine
Washable fabrics: Rinse in cold water and then wash using a biological detergent. Dried stains should be sponged with a white vinegar solution then the item should be soaked in a biological detergent before washing as normal.
Non-washable fabrics: Sponge fresh stains with warm, salty water then rinse and blot dry. If the stain is old, the item should be dry cleaned.

Vomit
Washable fabrics: Remove the excess and rinse well under cold water. Soak the item in warm water and biological detergent, then wash using a fresh detergent solution.
Non-washable fabrics: Remove the excess and sponge with warm water using a few drops of ammonia. Blot the area dry and repeat as necessary until all traces of the stain are removed.

INDEX